To Follow in Jesus' Steps

C. Wayne Zunkel

BRETHREN PRESS
Elgin, Illinois

To Follow in Jesus' Steps

A Manual for Participation in the Church of the Brethren

Copyright © 1991 by C. Wayne Zunkel

Brethren Press, 1451 Dundee Avenue, Elgin, IL 60120

Cover Illustration by Perry Board
Cover Design by Chris Paschen

Library of Congress Cataloging in Publication Data

Zunkel, C. Wayne.
    To follow in Jesus' steps.
    Bibliography: 1. Church of the Brethren—Doctrines—Handbooks, manuals, etc. I. Church of the Brethren. Parish Ministries Commission. II. Title.
    BX7821.2.Z86 1985   286'.5 85-5271
    ISBN 0-87178-847-0

Manufactured in the United States of America

"It was to this God called you,
for Christ himself suffered for you
and left you an example,
so that you would follow in his steps."
—1 Peter 2:21

Contents

Introduction

A Korean pastor, Dan Kim, walked into my office at the Panorama City (Los Angeles) Church one day some ten years ago. He wanted a place for his small Korean church to meet. In time, I asked him and his congregation to become a part of the Church of the Brethren. We had shared in Bible study, worship services, and the Love Feast several times. He said, "I think I know some of what the Brethren believe. But tell me again so I am certain."

To Follow in Jesus' Steps was first written for the "new Brethren," people like Dan Kim who come without any background for knowing who we are. I tried to sift through all that are cultural and discardable trimmings and get back to what is basic for us. (*Robert's Rules of Order*, for example, so dear to Brethren, actually does not appear in scriptures!) I tried to write as simply and directly as possible, without cutting any corners or softening any difficult beliefs, to simply put it out for him (and many others like him) to accept or reject.

In the deepest sense, there are no "Brethren beliefs." The Church of the Brethren is committed to the New Testament as its rule of faith and practice. If a belief is only "Brethren" it is unimportant.

Many people have contributed to this book, read manuscripts, and made suggestions. Unsolicited suggestions and reactions have come from all parts of our denomination. Various persons submitted the study materials they prepared to use with the book. For these we are grateful.

This expanded version of *To Follow in Jesus' Steps* is for all Brethren, new and old, urban and rural, educated and simple, black and white, brown, yellow, and red. But it is dedicated to the "new Brethren" among us—to those who come from other traditions and other cultures, even from other nations. They bring at least as much as they receive. Because of them, the Church of the Brethren has an infusion of new life, new enthusiasm and dedication, and a deeper understanding of the Christ who calls us to "come follow." Who knows, the next century may be the best century of all in terms of realizing just how precious is the treasure that has been entrusted to us!

C. Wayne Zunkel
Panorama City, California

1

Counting the Cost

In the late summer of 1708, **Alexander Mack** walked down into the waters of the Eder River near the little village of Schwarzenau, Germany, and was baptized. He in turn baptized his wife, Anna, and six others who had been meeting together for several years for prayer and study of the Scriptures. The group known today as the Church of the Brethren was born.

Mack was 29 years old. His father, John Philip Mack, was a prominent miller and businessman in his own village and an elder in the Reformed church. He had served two terms as mayor. Because of the course Alexander had set for his life, he would eventually lose most of his wealth and end up a refugee in an area of religious freedom, William Penn's colony, Pennsylvania, in what became the United States.

No Creed But Christ

The little group began in a land where there had been thirty years of war over religion. Catholics, Lutherans, and Reformed had killed and tortured one another over creeds. The army of one of the church-states would sweep over an area and force all the inhabitants to become a part of their church. Then another army would come and claim the area for another church.

Many of the common people began to feel they wanted nothing to do with any church.

The established churches had grown rich, powerful, and corrupt. They no longer shared the simple message of the New Testament and of Jesus.

Alexander Mack's own teacher, Ernst Christoph Hochmann von Hochenau, felt he could be a better Christian outside the church.

But young Mack and the little group of eight felt there must be a church—a church like the church in the New Testament. They set out to form such a church, taking **the New Testament as their rule of faith and practice**. In an age of killing over Christian creeds, they vowed to have **no creed but Christ**.

Some theologians may argue that a person is not a creed. But in saying "no creed but Christ," the early Brethren were insisting that to be a Christian involves more than correctly repeating the words of a formal statement. Brethren wanted the Word—Christ Jesus—to live in them!

The violence of Christians toward each other and toward others was repulsive to them. The conviction that there must be **no force in religion** was very important to them.

Worship was important to them. Study of the Scriptures was important to them. Being a part of a church was important to them. But as important as anything to them was a burning desire **to take Jesus very seriously**, to believe that Jesus was their Lord and Savior as Scripture presents him, to do what Jesus asked, to go where Jesus would send them, and to live, in accordance with his teachings, the kind of life he shared.

They were **primitive Christians**, trying to go back to the very beginnings of their faith.

To Follow in His Steps

Jesus called Matthew to leave his tax desk and come and follow. Matthew left his job, his friends, his old life and went with Jesus (Matthew 9:9).

Jesus called Simon Peter from his fishing nets and Peter left his wife, his family, his nets. Peter left everything and went with Jesus (Mark 1:16–18).

Peter went not knowing where Jesus would take him or what it would cost. But he loved and trusted Jesus. And he went discovering anew each day what following Jesus would mean.

Brethren believe that to be a Christian is not first of all a formal creed. Nor is it first of all a structured way to live—a list of do's and don'ts.

Beliefs and ethics will follow, but being a Christian begins with hearing Christ's call and saying "yes." What we understand when we begin will grow and develop as we go along.

To Count the Cost

The early Brethren were serious students of the Bible. They were not formally educated but were eager to learn at every opportunity.

Gottfried Arnold has been called the "idea father" of the Church of the Brethren because his works were studied and valued by Mack and the early leaders.

One of Arnold's works was called *The Impartial History of the Church and Heresies*. It is considered to be the first example of church history in a modern sense because Arnold went back to original sources to document what he had to say and didn't simply accept the judgment of the official church scholars at face value.

Gottfried Arnold's book argues that many times the heretics, ridiculed, tortured, driven from the church, burned at the stake, were more nearly right than was the institutional church that punished them.

The word *heretic* originally meant "to choose." The early Brethren suffered for insisting on their right "to choose," to be open to God's leading as they studied the Scriptures and tried to be faithful to Jesus.

A very important scripture for the early Brethren was Jesus' caution that those who would follow him ought to first "count the cost" (Luke 14:25–33). Their faith led to loss of home and property for some, division from family for others, and even prison and physical suffering, being sold as galley slaves and chained to an oar of a ship for a few. Because of this, it was important that no one take lightly the acceptance of the way of Christ.

To accept Christ is not only something we say with our lips or a feeling we have in our hearts. It **involves our very lives—all of us** (Matt. 7:21–22). Therefore, it is important that we carefully consider the step we are taking.

As we come to the Scriptures our question must not be "What will others think?", or "What might it cost?" but only "What is Jesus saying? What does God want of me?"

We Are Not Alone

Fortunately, we do not come to these questions alone. God's own Holy Spirit goes with us to guide us and strengthen us. We also have the fellowship and support of the family of the Church.

We are not born and left like orphans on a doorstep. The New Testament made it clear that we are born as Christians into a family of other Christians.

As we begin to learn to walk and talk as "babies in Jesus," at first we will eat baby food (1 Cor. 3:1–2). But others, older or more mature in the faith, will be with us. Together we learn and grow. Together we challenge each other to discover in our own time and place, to discover in our own life and experience, just what it is that God would have us do and how God would have us live.

For Brethren, the church fellowship is very important. It is as difficult to survive alone as a "babe in Christ" as it is to survive alone as a physical baby left unattended at birth in this world.

Unifying Themes

Across its history since 1708 and around the world today, individual members and congregations of the Church of the Brethren would not all seem the same. During periods of extravagance in society in its early days, the Brethren chose to wear the plain clothes of the Mennonites and Quakers as a witness for the simplicity they found taught by Jesus. Today there are differences of theology and worship forms in our congregations.

But there are some things which are important to us all. We will look at some of these together. But one of the deep, unifying convictions is the attempt to return to Jesus and let him be Lord and Savior of our own personal lives and, beyond that, Lord of every relationship and responsibility in the world.

The entire world belongs to God. As followers of Jesus we must seek God's will for every area of life.

To do: This week take one risk for your faith. Do something right which could involve being criticized or which could cost you something.

Some scriptures . . .

Follow in his steps—1 Peter 2:21
Count the cost—Luke 14:25–33
Not with our lips but with our lives as well—
Matthew 7:21–29
A part of one body—Romans 12:3–8
We begin as babies, but . . . —1 Corinthians 3:1–9
Come, follow me—Matthew 4:18–22

For further reading . . .

Emmert F. Bittinger, *Heritage and Promise*, 1983: Brethren Press, Elgin, Illinois.

Samuel Longenecker, *The Way, The Truth and The Life: Study Manual in Christian Doctrine*, a small pamphlet which lists Brethren emphases with scriptural references. Available from Brethren Press, Elgin, Illinois.

Graydon F. Snyder and Kenneth F. Shaffer, Jr., *Texts in Transit: A Study of New Testament Passages that Shaped the Brethren*, 1976. Brethren Press, Elgin, Illinois.

2

Gathered
Around the Word

We begin with Jesus.
   Some groups begin with Old Testament law. Some begin with the Apostle Paul. Some begin with the accumulated teachings of the church. Some begin with a set of "spiritual laws" about God's plan of salvation or with a set of "fundamentals."

Brethren begin with Jesus.

Jesus is the center of our faith. He is the beginning point and the end of all that we believe (Rev. 1:8; 21:6; 22:13).

Brethren believe that Jesus must be Lord of our lives.

When Jesus touches the lives of people they are better. People weighed down with sin find new life because of him.

Jesus is Lord. Jesus is also Savior.

Our Lord

On a clear night we can look up and see the stars and if we understand what we see, we can find our way.

On a cloudy night, we cannot see the stars. When the stars are hidden from our view, we need a compass.

Jesus is like a compass. In the midst of lives sometimes overwhelmed by passions of hatred or fear or lust, we cannot see clearly. Jesus points the way.

The first minister of the Brethren, Alexander Mack, said:

> It is, therefore, very good to look wholly and alone to the express words of the Lord Jesus, and to his own perfect example, and to follow that only . . . .

Our Savior

The Bible speaks of *blood* cleansing us from sin. Many hymns talk of being washed in the blood. The book of Revelation (7:14) says a multitude "have washed their robes and made them white in the blood of the Lamb."

We think of blood as staining. But medical science knows that, in the body, blood is a cleansing agent. It releases cargoes of fresh oxygen and absorbs waste products. Christ's blood, his life poured out, his love even to a cross is a cleansing agent for our world and for us, personally. In the cross we see the extent of God's love for us. At the foot of the cross we find forgiveness and cleansing and receive new life.

Both

Because Brethren believe strongly that Jesus is both Lord and Savior, they have a strong evangelical faith and strong social concern like that of the One they seek to serve. They note Ephesians 2:8 and 9 which remind us that "it is by grace" that we have been saved "through faith." But they continue reading that passage which, in verse 10, reminds us that we were "created in Christ Jesus for good works."Because both convictions run strong for the Brethren, they seem a puzzle to some Christians who want to focus on one or the other.

Forerunners of Faith

Ancestors of the Brethren are to be found in earlier Church history. Brethren historian Floyd Mallott, a generation ago, said the most important words he ever wrote were several pages in his book, *Studies in Brethren History*. He said the idea of the *imitation of Christ*, at the heart of Brethren beliefs, is to be found in earlier voices in the Christian church. Mallott lists three forerunners of the Brethren.

Bernard of Clairvaux was a great thinker. For a thousand years Jesus had been worshiped as the second person of the Trinity, the eucharistic Christ of the altar. But Bernard discovered Jesus, the Man of Nazareth, our companion, brother, teacher and example.

Francis of Assisi was neither a great scholar nor an organizer, but he gave his whole energy to living like Jesus. He gave away his wealth and married "lady poverty" and learned to love all people.

Peter Waldo, the closest ancestor of the Brethren, brought a practical, devout attitude, not determined by scholastic theory or doctrine of inspiration.

These three were motivated by no theory of the New Testament. They took it as the book that presented a picture of Jesus and of primitive Christianity.

Wherever Christianity like that of Bernard and Francis and Waldo has appeared it has been different. It has been concerned about **how we live** and relate to people. It has been **democratic**, involving the laity in its decisions. It has been willing to go **against the culture** and the nation where it finds itself in opposition because of its determination to be faithful to Jesus. To accept Jesus as the Lord of our lives and as our Savior are twin convictions on which the Brethren base their faith.

The Whole Bible

For Brethren, the entire Bible is important. It is the setting in which God speaks. It is God's love letter to people. The Bible is important because of Jesus. It provides for us the background, the setting into which Jesus came. We cannot fully understand Jesus apart from the Bible. The themes of Jesus' life begin in the earliest passages of Genesis and are traced through the entire Old Testament. The Old Covenant prepares the way for the New.

The New Testament is important because of the closeness in time of its writings to Jesus. A beloved Bible teacher among the Brethren, Carl Zeigler, loved to quote Floyd Mallott regarding the Bible: "The 'new' is in the 'old' concealed. The 'old' is in the 'new' revealed."

A People of the Book

Bible study has been important for the Brethren. The early Brethren began out of a period of very serious Bible study.

The early Brethren shared in serious group Bible study years before the Sunday school movement began to sweep across early America.

At our denominational Annual Conference, early morning Bible study is an important ingredient. Morning business sessions are arranged so that the entire delegate body and observers may share in mass Bible study. Items of business regarding church life and witness are preceded by a scriptural background.

A careful, in-depth study of the Bible is widely used by Brethren congregations through a three-year program called **People of the Covenant**. The study is biblical and interpersonal. It stresses the covenant nature of faith—that our faith involves making promises to each other and to God. It focuses on us, on the needs around us, and on our world. Those who study are led to try to practice what they learn in their study of the Bible.

Letting the Bible Speak to Us

Some Christian groups argue over the inerrancy of the Scriptures, that is, whether every word in the Bible was dictated by God.

Brethren tended to avoid such debates. Being of German background, from the earliest days they knew the little differences between German language and English language Bibles. The Bible was the Word of God, yes. And inspired by God, yes, and to be handled with great care and reverence.

Brethren took the Bible very seriously. In a way they were literalists in the best sense of that word. Their literal reading of the Sermon on the Mount shaped their dedication to peace, their resistance to going to war, and their refusal to take oaths.

They knew in their own experience that the translations we hold in our hands are not the original manuscripts. They learned to look for the divine message of God, not to get mired down in individual words or phrases.

More than that, Brethren have always taken seriously the New Testament conviction that Jesus is himself *the Word made flesh* (John 1:14). Jesus said to some who came to him: "You search the Scriptures because you think that in them you have eternal life. And they do bear witness to me. Yet you fail to come to me that you may have life" (John 5:39).

Their attitude was captured by the words of the hymn: "Beyond the sacred page, I seek Thee, Lord."

Latter-Day Scriptures

Brethren would not accept the attempts of some groups to "go beyond Jesus" with holy writings which pretend to supplement or supersede Jesus. Any truth about God will be in keeping with the truth Christ revealed. Jesus is "the way, the truth and the life" (John 14:6). Jesus is the alpha and the omega, the "a" and the "z" of our faith, the beginning point and the conclusion. Others may illuminate what Jesus taught, but none will ever go beyond.

Because They Had Known Persecution

As we noted in chapter one, early in their history, the Brethren were persecuted by other Christians because their beliefs were different. They were imprisoned, whipped, and chained to oars as galley slaves. Because of this, Brethren never persecuted anyone else.

Many Brethren are grateful for the freedom which our church has given them to work their way through to a meaningful faith. Some have said, "If it had not been for that accepting spirit, I probably would not be a part of any church today."

Through What Eyes?

We all read with a point of view. None of us is entirely objective. Brethren believe the Old Testament must be read in light of the teachings of the New Testament. They believe that the New Testament must be read in light of the Gospels. They believe that we must read the Gospels in the light of Christ, his mind and his spirit.

We begin with Jesus.

To do: This week read the Gospel of Matthew. Keep notes on what you think God would have you do if you were to take Christ seriously.

Some scriptures . . .

Beyond the sacred page—John 5:37–40
Jesus himself is the Word—John, chapter 1
Work out your own salvation—Philippians 2:12–13
All Scripture is helpful—2 Timothy 3:16–17

Be like the Bereans—Acts 17:10–11
God's Word in our hearts—Jeremiah 31:31–34

For further reading . . .

Martin G. Brumbaugh, *A History of the Brethren*, the Brethren Publishing House, 1899, pp. 1-11.

Floyd E. Mallott, *Studies in Brethren History*, House of the Church of the Brethren, 1954, pages 17-20.

Donald F. Durnbaugh, "Sunday School Movement," *The Brethren Encyclopedia*, Volume 2, K–Z, The Brethren Encyclopedia, 1983, pages 1237–1239.

3

Believer's Baptism

In 1708, when the Brethren began, people throughout Europe automatically were baptized as babies into the ruling state church. To be a citizen of the state was to be a Christian. Today in some countries there are still state churches.

The early Brethren read the words of Jesus, "believe and be baptized" (Mark 16:16; Acts 18:8). They asked, "How can a little baby believe?" They saw the Christian life as something a person **chooses** to do, not something one automatically is because of a ritual that has been performed by someone else.

Two groups greatly influenced the early Brethren. One was the **Pietists**, mostly people trying to reform the existing churches from within. They were devoted to prayer, Bible study, greater lay participation, and the focusing of the church's message on the spiritual and day-to-day needs of people, rather than on dry dogma.

The other group which began in the 1600s was called **Anabaptists**, which means "rebaptizers." They had all been baptized as babies into one of the state churches but insisted on **believers' baptism** as an evidence of their own desire to accept Christ and walk in his way. But, in that day, to be baptized a second time was a crime punishable by death.

Even though the early Protestant reformers, including Martin Luther, had explored the possibility of believers' baptism instead of infant baptism, they decided against it and became violently opposed to it. In Switzerland, persons found guilty of the "crime" of rebaptism were executed by drowning as a way of mocking the immersion baptism practiced.

The early Brethren, as they studied the Scriptures, discovered that the word for baptism in the Greek meant "to be immersed."

They noted that Jesus went down into the Jordan River (Matt. 3:13–16) when he was baptized. The book of Acts told of Philip looking for a body of water so that he might take the Ethiopian eunuch down into it for baptism (Acts 8:38).

The early church practiced immersion baptism of believers. But along the way, church leaders said that to sprinkle water on the head was enough.

The early Brethren believed that committing the head is not enough. We must give over all of life. God wants all of us. At great cost, they returned to the New Testament practice of believer's baptism, immersion baptism, which represented being completely surrounded by the will and purpose of God.

They rejected the traditional view of sacrament where God's grace is mediated regardless of the attitude of the priest or of the worshipper if the ritual is properly performed and if the formula is recited properly.

Baptism and communion are not like a spiritual aspirin which magically takes effect. They are outward symbols of a reality that is happening within. No one else can do this for you. The Old Testament book of Ezekiel rejected an old Hebrew idea that the children are punished for the sins of their parents and that parents are punished for the sins of their children (Ezekiel 18).

Ezekiel said that children are punished for their own sins, and that parents are punished for their own sins. We all stand before God alone. Each of us must first make the choice as to what life for us shall be.

But once we make that decision, we are not left alone. As we make it, we want to symbolize it through a public act of being baptized.

Baptism represents **cleansing** from our past life. All that has been wrong is washed away. We emerge from the baptismal waters washed clean.

Baptism represents **commitment**. It represents our willingness to give over all of life to God as we have come to know God through Jesus.

Baptism and the laying on of hands after baptism represent the opening of our heart **to receive God's Holy Spirit**, which will be with us and attend us (Acts 2:38).

Baptism represents **acceptance into a new family** as full sons and daughters. We no longer are alone in any sense. We are family now, full participants in the family of those who have privately and publicly dedicated life to God (Romans 8:17).

Three Questions

Three questions are asked at baptism:

"Do you believe that Jesus is God's son and that he brought to earth a saving gospel?"

"Do you willingly turn from sin and, with God's help, do you seek to live according to the example and teaching of Jesus Christ?"

"Do you give yourself to the Church? Do you promise to uphold it with your prayers, your presence, your service, your substance?"

If the person answers those questions "yes," the pastor says, "I baptize you in the name of the Father and of the Son and of the Holy Spirit," using the formula which Jesus gave in his great commission as he sent his disciples out before his ascension (Matthew 28:19).

The applicant is kneeling in water which comes to the shoulders. As the pastor says those words, the applicant's head is brought forward three times. For many there is a feeling of great **release**. Burdens carried over many years may suddenly be lifted. For many, younger and older, **a new joy** comes to the heart. There is the feeling of **being clean**—truly clean—on the inside and on the outside for the first time in their lives. For many there comes a **happiness** and a **peace** which the world cannot give. Neither can the world take it away (John 14:27).

Then, with the applicant still kneeling, the pastor gently lays hands on the head of the applicant, one hand over the other, and offers a prayer for that person. The laying on of hands is an ancient symbol of being endowed by God's Spirit.

After that, as the person stands, the pastor greets the new Christian with a handshake or an embrace. The applicant has entered the water and been baptized in a manner which the Scriptures describe as "dying to the old self" (Romans 6:3–11). The past is buried. Old mistakes are buried. Life is handed over completely to God. The new Christian rises to life with a peace and a power which do not come from our own efforts.

Brethren **receive** people from other Christian churches without requiring rebaptism if those who come are satisfied with their former baptism. But Brethren only **baptize** believers by trine immersion.

With Some Cost

Many early Brethren insisted on baptism in flowing streams since Christ was baptized in a flowing stream. Sometimes this took place in the cold of winter. The first baptisms in the United States were in the Wissahickon Creek near Germantown, Pennsylvania, in what is today inner-city Philadelphia. They took place on December 25, 1723. In those early days Brethren actually broke the ice in order to baptize.

Today Brethren churches have baptistries in their church buildings. But some still choose to be baptized in a flowing stream, in a lake, or in the ocean.

When Saint Patrick was evangelizing the British Isles, the story is told of his baptizing an old Celtic chieftain. They had gone down into a rapidly flowing stream. To keep his balance, according to the story, Saint Patrick drove his staff hard into the river bed. When he had finished, Saint Patrick noticed a red stain in the water around the staff. To his dismay, he realized that he had driven his staff through the leg of the old chief. He began to apologize. The chief replied, "Oh, I thought it was all a part of the ceremony."

Jesus never promised that following him would be easy. Baptism represents our willingness to "count the cost" and go with him. Baptism represents newness of life. The Scriptures say, "The old things have passed away; behold, they are become new" (2 Corinthians 5:17).

At baptism, we no longer meet life alone. God goes with us in a new way. And in a new way we have a family of brothers and sisters who have also committed their lives as we have, and they go with us wherever our faith takes us.

Child Dedication

Instead of baptizing babies, Brethren bring their infants to church for a service of dedication. As the mother Hannah brought her newly weaned son Samuel to the house of God for dedication (1 Sam. 1:22–28), as Mary and Joseph took the child Jesus to the temple to be dedicated to God (Luke 2:22–24), so Brethren have tried to follow the Biblical pattern.

Services of child dedication may be held near Christmas or Mother's Day—at least twice a year—and at other times when parents request it.

The babies are brought to the front of the church by their parents who stand before the pastor. Often another couple or individual stands with the parents, much as godparents do in infant baptism.

The pastor reads scripture or offers an appropriate poem and tells the purpose of the event. Parents are asked to renew their own dedication to God, their commitment to each other to build a strong home, and their commitment to the church to draw upon its resources as they raise their child. They are asked if they now present their child to God for dedication. The entire congregation may be asked if they will undergird these parents with prayer and support.

The pastor places a hand upon the head of each child and, calling the child by name, says, " _____ , I dedicate you to God, in the name of the Father and of the Son and of the Holy Spirit." A prayer of consecration is offered for all the children being dedicated. Sometimes each mother is presented with a rose or carnation.

In many ways, the service of child dedication is more a service of parent rededication. It is also a time when the congregation is reminded that this larger Christian family shares in the task of raising children of God who are whole and well.

To do: Ask forgiveness of someone you have wronged and do your part to make things right.

Some scriptures . . .

The great commission—Matthew 28:18–20
What shall we do?—Acts 2:37–38
Immersion baptism—Acts 8:26–40
Dying to the old, resurrected to new life—Romans 6:1–11

Jesus blessing the children—Matthew 19:13–15; Mark 10:13–16; Luke 18:15–17

For further reading . . .

William M. Beahm, *The Meaning of Baptism*, The Brethren Press, Elgin, Illinois.

Vernard M. Eller, "The Theology of Baptism," *The Brethren Encyclopedia*, Donald F. Durnbaugh, editor, 1983, vol. 1, pp. 82–86.

4

The Love Feast

On the night that Jesus was arrested and tried and sentenced to be crucified, he wanted one last meal with his disciples. Eating together is always important for friends. This last meal was to be a special time to share the deepest longings of his heart before he would be taken from them (Luke 22:14).

The Washing of Feet

Jesus had secured a rented room. The meal was prepared. But as the disciples arrived, they came in arguing over who would sit next to Jesus and over who would be first in his coming kingdom (Luke 22:24–27).

Through all of his time with them, Jesus had tried to teach them that they were not to live like pagans. They were to be servants of one another. They were to be loving and humble (Matt. 20:20–28). Yet with his time with them almost gone, they were spending the last few precious moments fighting like children.

It was the custom in those days for a slave to wash the feet of guests as they entered a home. The roads were hot and dusty. They all wore sandals. Their feet were very tired. To have a servant wash your feet was to feel refreshed and welcomed. In that rented upper room, a basin and towel had been provided. But there was no servant to wash their feet.

Instead of trying to talk further about lessons he had been talking about for three years, Jesus quietly rose from the table, tied the towel around his waist, took the basin, knelt down and began, one by one, to wash their feet (John 13:17). They were shocked. But none of them said a word until Jesus came to Simon Peter. Peter often blurted out what the rest of them were feeling.

Simon Peter said to Jesus, "You will never wash my feet!"

Jesus looked up into Peter's eyes and said, "If I do not wash your feet, you have no part with me."

Peter said, "Well then, not my feet only, but also my hands and my head."

Jesus said to Peter, "The feet are enough."

When he had completed his task and had returned the basin and the towel to their place, he sat down. He said to them, "Do you know what I have done? You call me teacher and Lord, and you are right, for so I am. If I, your Lord and teacher, have washed your feet, you also should wash one another's feet, for I have given you an example that you should do as I have done to you."

For them it was both an experience of cleansing and a calling for them to be servants to one another and to anyone in need. It represented a cleansing of the sin of pride and self-centeredness.

The Agapé Meal

Before them on the table that evening was a meal. They ate together.

In the Middle East, to eat together was to symbolize a special bond. They did not eat with strangers. In the Old Testament, Lot invited two strangers into his home. His servants washed their feet. He made a feast and baked unleavened bread. After they had eaten together, Lot discovered that they were in danger and he defended the strangers with his life (Genesis 19).

Jesus wanted to eat together with the disciples that night because he knew how much they would need each other in the days ahead. Their common meal also commemorated the love and joy that marked their fellowship and kept them reminded of the great wedding supper of the Lamb toward which they were headed.

Many times the early church ate together as they met together. Because they ate together, because they prayed and sang together, they were able to suffer and die together when their faith made high demands (Acts 2:43–47).

The Bread And The Cup

The Gospels disagree as to whether the Last Supper took place on the night of the celebration of the Jewish Passover (John 13:1, Luke 22:1, Mark 14:12–16, Matt. 26:17). But the Gospels agree that elements of the Last Supper were similar to those of the Passover, although with a new meaning. The Passover celebrated Israel's freedom from the slavery of Egypt. The Last Supper celebrated a New Covenant, a new freedom in Christ.

On that table was unleavened bread and a cup. The Jewish unleavened bread, matzo, was a brittle cracker. Jesus took it and broke it. It snapped as he broke it.

He said to them, "This represents my body which will be broken." He had a broken piece in each hand, and after he had given thanks for it, he offered it to them.

"Take, eat" (Matthew 26:26).

They, too, were to join in the fellowship of his broken body. They, too, were to enter into his life of servanthood and suffering love.

Jesus took a cup from the table and said, "This cup represents my blood which will be poured out." After he blessed it, he offered it to them. "Drink of it, all of you" (Matt. 26:27). In the Bible, blood represents life (Lev. 17:11). The fruit of the vine in the cup represented his life, shed for them. He invited them to let his life, his love, his caring, his sacrifice live in them. His dreams were to fill their heads. His life was to consume their lives. His blood was to flow in their veins. They were to be his people in the world, carrying on his life-giving ministry.

Then they sang a hymn and went out (Matt. 26:30). Simon Peter went out to deny he ever knew his Lord. Judas went out to betray him. The others went out to forsake him in his hour of need. But the call was and is to go forth from those tables to love and serve him.

That He Might Live In Us

The elements of that evening were to be a **reminder**. Followers of Christ were to do those things "in remembrance of me,"

to recall his life, his teachings and his death "until he comes."
(1 Corinthians 11:23–26)

As the early Brethren opened their Bibles and attempted to
follow Jesus, they wanted to observe the Last Supper as Jesus
had shared it. **The love feast** (term from Jude 12) has had a
profound effect upon their lives. The world-wide service program of the Church of the Brethren, some have felt, grew out of
this experience together.

When **Martin Brumbaugh** was governor of Pennsylvania, he
returned to his home church in Middle Pennsylvania to wash
the feet of coal miners.

Andrew Cordier served as assistant to the Secretary-General
of the United Nations. Sometimes he was involved in around-
the-clock negotiations with the Russians.

Cordier was a careful and learned student of history. He was
skilled in negotiation and political science. But he said that
nothing prepared him for those tiring experiences like the love
feast as he had experienced it in his church in East Nimishillen,
Ohio. He talked of the "utter sincerity, utter fairness, and utter
integrity" which were necessary before coming to the Lord's
table. Through foot washing he had learned to relate to others
in a spirit of humility and love.

Reliving Those Moments

Many Brethren churches observe a bread and cup communion throughout the year. But on Thursday of Holy Week or Palm
Sunday and, for many, on World Communion Sunday, the first
Sunday in October, most Brethren churches observe the full love
feast.

Usually the love feast is held in the early evening. Candles
are sometimes used on the tables to give the semi-darkened
room a soft light. In some churches tables are divided with men
at some tables and women at others.

Often there will be an opening hymn and some words of
preparation and a prayer. Someone will be asked to read the
passage from John 13 which tells of Jesus washing the feet of his
disciples. Sometimes the leader will talk about what this can
mean in our lives.

Footwashing tubs with warm water are placed along the table
with a towel to be tied around the waist. One person begins
washing the feet of the person seated next. When finished, both
will stand and they will embrace and kiss each other on the

cheek. Often they exchange words of Christian encouragement such as "God bless you."

Then the person whose feet have been washed, in turn washes the feet of the next person. This continues until all have had the experience both of washing feet and of having feet washed. Many times hymns are sung from memory as this part of the service occurs.

Following the feetwashing service, a scripture is read about the meal. Sometimes John 15:1–5 is used. A prayer is offered for the meal. A simple meal is served. Sometimes this includes beef and a soup of broth. Sometimes the hymn "Blest Be the Tie That Binds" is sung.

Scriptural background for the bread and cup is read. A prayer for the bread is offered. The Apostle Paul asked the question, "The bread which we break, is it not the communion of the body of Christ?" (1 Corinthians 10:16). Brethren sometimes use this as an affirmation as they hold the piece of unleavened bread across the table with the person opposite them. As they break the bread, they say together, "This bread which we break is the communion of the body of Christ." Communion means to be "one with Christ."

After a few moments of meditation, a prayer of blessing is offered for the cup.

Earlier Brethren used a common cup. Sometimes today individual cups may be placed on the table.

As the cup is held, Brethren again make a positive statement out of the Apostle Paul's question. They say together, "This cup of the New Covenant is the communion of the blood of Christ."

Often the participants will then share in a closing prayer, sing a hymn, and go out in a spirit of reverence.

Sometimes in the services a choir will sing or solos related to the Last Supper or to Christ's suffering and death will be sung. Usually an attempt is made to include different people in the reading of Scripture.

For many Brethren, the celebration of the love feast is one of the most important events together. Often more people take part in this event than in Easter or Christmas services.

In most cases, the Lord's table is open to any Christian who wants to share. We do not come to the table because we are worthy. We come because we are human and frail and we need the forgiveness, the strengthening, and the love which Christ offers. We come as imperfect people who need the blessing which is offered here.

Brethren have found the Lord's promise true: "If you know these things, blessed are you if you do them" (John 13:17). Their lives have been enriched.

To do: Find a way to serve without being noticed. (One time I saw the great Christian Toyohiko Kagawa lingering behind to pick up the paper towels off the floor of the restroom. He was about to address a large audience at Manchester College, but he took time to be an almost unnoticed servant.)

Some scriptures ...

The mood of the disciples—Luke 22:24–27
The response of Jesus—John 13:1–17
Meals of love in the early church—Acts 2:43–47
The blessing is not automatic—1 Corinthians 11:23–34

For further reading ...

William M. Beahm, *The Brethren Love Feast*, Brethren Press, Elgin, Illinois.

Graydon Snyder, "Love Feast," in *The Brethren Encyclopedia*, Donald Durnbaugh, editor, 1983, pp. 762–764.

5

Anointing for Healing

When Jesus sent out his disciples, they were told to preach and teach and "anoint with oil" those that were sick (Mark 6:12).

James 5, verses 13 and following, tells early Christians that if any are sick they are to call for the elders of the church "and let them pray over him, anointing him with oil in the name of the Lord; and the prayer of faith will save the sick man, and the Lord will raise him up; and if he has committed sins, he will be forgiven. Therefore, confess your sins to one another and pray for one another that you may be healed. The prayer of a righteous man has great power in its effects."

Olive oil had symbolic meaning for the Jews. In the Old Testament it represented God's election. The kings were anointed when they took office. They knelt down and oil was placed on their heads to symbolize that God had chosen them to serve him and the people (1 Samuel 10:1, 15:1, 16:1–13, 2 Kings 11:12).

The term Christ or Messiah meant "anointed one." Jesus was one chosen by God to be his anointed one. Psalm 23 says: "He anointeth my head with oil, my cup overflows" (v. 5).

Oil also represented healing. The story of the Good Samaritan tells of the Samaritan tending to the wounds of the victim along the road, pouring on oil. (Luke 10:34)

The service of anointing as shared by Christ was practiced by the Christian church until the eighth century and then lost. It began to be observed only as last rites for the dead.

When Pope John XXIII threw open the windows of his Roman Catholic Church and Catholic scholars began to open the Scriptures in a new way, they became convinced that anointing as shared in the New Testament was not a service for the dead but a service for healing and life, and they began to recover that ancient practice.

Anointing Today

As practiced by Brethren, a person who is sick or who faces serious surgery may ask to be anointed. A pastor or deacon or lay person may participate in the service.

On occasion anointing may be done at a public service, but usually the service is very personal and includes only close friends or the immediate family.

A scripture is read: Psalm 23 or Psalm 139 which says that God has made us and knows us better than we can know ourselves, or Romans 8:18–39 which reminds us that "in everything God works for good with those who love him, who are called according to his purpose," or the passage from James 5.

The person in charge may share what anointing means. Those present may talk about experiences which they or others have had.

Opportunity is given for the one to be anointed to share any feelings. Sometimes the question is asked, "Is there anything in your life that might prevent healing? Are there concerns you have or fears or burdens that you carry or sins which you feel have not been forgiven?"

Sometimes the sick person asks everyone but the person in charge to leave the room and then shares a particular burden which has been carried within.

After this time of sharing, a few drops of olive oil are placed on the leader's hand. With a few fingers dipped in the oil, the oil is then placed on the forehead of the one anointed.

The leader says, "I anoint you for the forgiveness of sin," placing the oil on the forehead, "For the increase of faith," placing oil again on the forehead, "And for the restoration of health," again placing oil on the forehead.

Then the leader and another person lay hands lightly on the forehead and each offers a prayer.

The prayer lifts up the special needs of the person. It may ask that all that prevents healing be swept away. It places the person's life fully in the hands of God, to trust God for healing and strength.

Toward Wholeness

The Greek word for "salvation" means wholeness. To be saved is to be whole, healed, well.

Sometimes wholeness comes to a sick person's life even though that person may die physically. But there is complete peace and acceptance within.

I shared one time in the anointing for a person who had been a Christian leader. He was near death. When the time for sharing came, he asked everyone else to leave the room. Then he shared some deep bitterness which he had carried in his heart for many years. The bitterness had gnawed away at him and sapped his strength.

After he shared and emptied out the spiritual poisons, we talked and prayed together. He knew that his life was now free of that pain. He knew that he was right with God. He was at peace.

As a matter of fact, he died within a matter of weeks. But he died whole and well before God.

If we hold a straw parallel to the Gulf Stream, the mighty Gulf Stream will flow through it. If we get our lives in line with the will and power of God, the very love and power of God will flow through them.

When we face an operation, we may be tense and understandably nervous. Nurses can give us medicine to make us sleep. But they cannot relax the worried mind and the tense muscles.

A woman in her eighties during her life had been operated on many times. Before each of these operations she experienced the anointing.

Surgeons who never knew her commented later that they never operated on anyone who was so relaxed.

Doctors do not heal us. Doctors and medical science play an important role in healing. God gave us minds and expects us to use them. But doctors do not heal.

Doctors can create conditions where healing can take place. They can set a broken bone. They can stitch torn skin. They can remove a tumor. But the knitting of the bone or the healing of the cut or the restoring of the body after the removal of a growth is something no doctor, however skilled, can do.

God gives the healing.

Medical science now knows that there are factors within us which can prevent healing. There is garbage in our lives which prevents the free flow of God's healing power.

We are each **one person,** body, mind, and soul. Physical illness can affect the mental outlook. Sometimes people who are dying a slow, painful death find their whole world is clouded. Once-kind people can sometimes become impatient and angry.

Spiritual problems and mental turmoil can affect physical health.

In our time of physical need we must draw on all the resources made available to us. We need all the understanding which medical science can give us. We need all the insights into the human mind and its workings that are available.

We need to draw on the rich spiritual resources which God puts in our hands.

Anointing is **visualized prayer.** It is a way of outwardly symbolizing the great strength that can be ours. It is not magic. It is a spiritual gift—similar to baptism and communion.

Anointing is not the same as "faith healing" which attempts to make medical science unnecessary.

Accepting the Blessings

And yet miraculous results sometimes come from anointing. Doctors simply say that they have done all they can. And good doctors acknowledge that there is more than their limited minds can know.

A young mother with rheumatoid arthritis was growing progressively worse. Her husband was an alcoholic and had left her many times. She was living alone with her small children.

The medical outlook was that she would become progressively crippled and unable to care for her children. There was fear, loneliness, anxiety, and anger.

In the anointing service, she shared her feelings openly and honestly. There was a sharing of fear and of faith. The prayer was not for simply physical healing but for healing first within the heart and mind. The woman opened her life to God in trust and love.

A few days later the attending physician remarked that he did not know what had happened but it seemed that the sickness was reversing itself. Within a matter of weeks the woman seemed totally well.

The poisons within herself, the emotional and spiritual blockages, were swept away. She was able to receive the healing which God had for her.

God wants for us far more than we want for ourselves. God loves us far more than we can love ourselves. The need is not to come to God to beg or plead. The need is to empty our hands, to let go of the things we cling to so tightly, in order that our hands and our lives will be open to receive the wonderfully amazing gifts God has to give.

The gifts are there. The blockage comes from within us.

To do: This week trust God in your life in one area where before you had held tight control.

Some scriptures . . .

Christ sends out the disciples to anoint—Mark 6:12
The early church practiced anointing—James 5:13–16
God has made us and knows us—Psalm 139
God wills the best for us—Romans 8:18–39

For further reading . . .

Harold Z. Bomberger, "Anointing," *The Brethren Encyclopedia,* Donald Durnbaugh, editor, Volume 1, 1983, pp. 39–40.

Warren D. Bowman, *Anointing for Healing,* Brethren Press, Elgin, Illinois.

Dean Miller, "Anointing," Brethren Press, Elgin, Illinois.

Graydon Snyder, "Anointing: A Bible Study," Brethren Press, Elgin, Illinois.

Leslie Weatherhead, *Psychology, Religion and Healing,* 1951: Abingdon Press, Nashville, Tennessee.

6

The Priesthood of All Believers

B rethren believe in the priesthood of all believers (1 Peter 2:9; Rev. 1:6; 5:10). We are to be priests (mediators of God's love and God's truth) to one another. We need each other if we are to discover and do God's will.

Jesus was very critical of the professional religious leaders of his day (Matt. 23). He was troubled by their elaborate religious dress and their insistence on honor and privilege. They wanted for themselves the best seats in the synagogues and salutations in the market place. They insisted on being called rabbi.

For Jesus' followers it was to be different. "You are not to be called rabbi, for you have one teacher and you are all brethren," he told them. "And call no man your father on earth, for you have one Father, who is in heaven. Neither be called masters, for you have one master, the Christ." Repeatedly he said to them, "He who is greatest among you shall be your servant; whoever exalts himself will be humbled and whoever humbles himself will be exalted." He totally reversed the modern notion of greatness.

There would be leaders in his church, of course. We have different gifts. Some of us can teach. Others can preach. Some have the gift of hospitality. Some have the gift of administration. Others are good at other things. We are all to discover our gift and to share it with the total body (1 Corinthians 12:4–30).

The gifts are not ours. They belong to the entire church. We have different roles to play in the work of Christ. But none of us is more important than another. Every gift and every role is important.

Some may be pastors or teachers or deacons. Some serve in other ways. But we all are involved in the work of ministry. We are all ministers. Minister means servant.

The Apostle Paul wrote in Ephesians 4 of these various gifts which he said are "for the equipment of the saints (every Christian), for the work of ministry, for building up the body of Christ until we all attain to the unity of the faith and of the knowledge of the Son of God, to maturity, to the measure of the stature of the fullness of Christ" (vs. 12 and 13).

There are to be no first and second class citizens in the kingdom of God. We are all citizens together, sojourners together in a shared journey.

The early Brethren places of worship were called "meeting houses." There was a reluctance to copy the elaborate cathedrals and costly churches of their day.

In their places of worship, the floor was level. The preacher was not elevated. Today most Brethren places of worship are like other Protestant churches, but the concern still exists.

Many Brethren pastors do not like the term *Reverend* which means "worthy of respect and worship." They prefer the term *Pastor*.

Many stress that **every member is a minister**. Every Christian had the laying on of hands at baptism and was "ordained" to share in the work of the ministry through the special gifts which each has been given by God.

Although there is a variety of dress, many Brethren pastors prefer not to wear a robe when preaching. Many choose to preach dressed in the garb of the people. Some will say frankly, "These clothes are my 'vestments.' I choose them carefully. I choose to dress like the worshipers to symbolize that we are one people." We have different gifts but we are all ministers together—priests to one another.

The Role of Women

The Church of the Brethren has taken seriously the Apostle Paul's declaration that in Christ there is "neither male nor female" (Gal. 3:28) but that we are all one.

Women were the first to the open tomb on Easter morning (Matt. 28:1). They were the first to announce the resurrection of Christ (Matt. 28:7–8).

Women gave leadership in the establishment of new churches (Acts 16:13–15). Women were evangelists in the New Testament church (Phil. 4:2–3).

Even though they came out of the German culture, which was male-dominated, the Brethren in the mid-1880s had a woman preacher, **Sarah Righter Major.**

Today women hold many leadership roles in the denomination. They serve on boards and committees and are often elected to chair these groups. Women sometimes serve as moderators of local congregations or of districts, even of Annual Conference.

There are women on the national staff at Elgin, Illinois, and in leadership positions there. A growing number of congregations have women as pastors.

Women are valued people within the life of the Church of the Brethren. At times Brethren have failed to live up to this ideal, but the commitment to the ideal is strong.

A Church of the People

The Church of the Brethren is organized to make use of the best thinking and contributions of all its members. Every member, new or long-term, young or old, rich or poor, white or yellow or red or brown or black, stands alongside every other member in the decisions that are made for the life and direction of the church.

Organization

In the Church of the Brethren the highest decision-making body is the **Annual Conference.** For Brethren it is the final authority on matters of practice and doctrine.

In the early years in the United States, Brethren who were scattered and facing the pressure of other religious groups decided to begin to come together on a regular, yearly basis.

Annual Conference is a time for doing business. Queries (questions) from congregations or from districts are considered and acted upon.

The Brethren practice "representative democracy" beyond the local church. Each congregation is permitted delegates in relationship to the size of that church.

Only delegates may vote, but anyone may attend. And anyone may speak in the business sessions. Entire families regularly make Annual Conference a time of inspiration, serious discussion, and vacation.

Prior to Annual Conference, a **standing committee** made up of delegates from each district reviews the business and suggests possible solutions. But Conference acting with Standing Committee in the general sessions is free to follow its own leading and often does.

Decisions of Annual Conference are not legally binding, but are offered as recommendations back to the congregations and the church at large.

Across the years it has seemed that the Spirit of God has moved among a prayerful, thoughtful delegate body and that the combined decision is wiser than any few congregations or individuals might have come to.

Many Brethren feel a special responsibility to abide by the decisions of Conference even when they are different from what they personally might have liked.

But the week-long (Tuesday night through Sunday for the actual Conference activities) meeting is more than the transaction of business. Each day begins with breakfast and post-breakfast meetings. Bible study is a central part of each morning. In the evening are mass worship experiences. Following the evening session there are late night groups focusing on many areas of the church's life.

And Annual Conference is more than inspiration. In the truest sense, Annual Conference is a massive **family reunion.** People from all walks of life within the church are bound together in sharing, a renewal of their own spiritual lives, and a renewal and deepening of their strong ties to one another. Much of the real business of Conference takes place outside the formal meetings, in the hallways and on the sidewalks as friends and Christian brothers and sisters from around the world share personal history and the deepest discoveries of their own faith journeys.

Annual Conference elects a **General Board** which meets several times throughout the year to carry out the worldwide program of the church as outlined by Annual Conference. The Board operates within a budget approved by the Conference.

The Board selects staff whose central headquarters are in Elgin, Illinois, although many staff members are assigned to posts across the United States and in many other countries.

There are no financial assessments which the denomination requires of the congregation each year. Instead, each congregation decides what it is able to give and informs the denomination and the district of this amount through a process of "self-allocation."

At the district level, decisions are made by a **District Conference** which meets annually. Again each congregation sends delegates depending on its size, but anyone may attend.

District Conferences each elect a **District Board** which implements the program set forth by District Conference and within a budget approved by District Conference.

Each district board will name staff to work full or part-time to help in the carrying out of its program. Each district has a district executive and secretarial help. Some have additional staff people in such areas as Christian education or new church development. The district staff assists congregations in securing pastoral leadership.

Each local church makes its major decisions in a **congregational business meeting** or church council. At such meetings every member has one vote, regardless of age or status.

Budget, pastoral leadership, congregational offices, building programs, all major decisions go to the congregational meeting.

Every local church elects its own **moderator** to preside at these meetings and to give organizational leadership.

Congregations have regularly scheduled business meetings several times a year but provide for special business meetings, with proper notice, as needed.

The congregational business meeting elects a **church board.** The board usually meets monthly and attends to the details of congregational life. Each board will have a chairperson. Each church selects other officers such as a treasurer and Sunday School personnel.

At every level, denominational, district and local, the boards divide into **commissions** which are responsible for specific tasks. The simplest division in the local church may be Stewards (responsible for the church plant and for finances), Witness (evangelism and service), and Nurture (Christian education and worship). National staff has World Ministries, Parish Ministries, and General Services Commissions. Basic decisions or recommendations are taken back to the board for action. And major decisions are taken to the larger body which elected them.

Some congregations coming into the Church of the Brethren may have a form of local church organization which is different from what has been described. Although congregations are urged to move in this direction, there is freedom in this area. An identical form of congregational life is not a precondition for being a part of the Church of the Brethren.

Pastors in the Church of the Brethren are not appointed by some bishop or district superintendent. Nor are they entirely the choice of the congregation.

The congregation may issue a call to a pastor and vote on that pastor. But the attempt always is to do this in consultation with the district executive and with ministerial personnel at the denominational level.

For Brethren, each local church is a part of a larger family. Congregations are free to develop their own programs as they see fit. But they are not isolated, entirely independent units. Our denominational policy is that local property is held in trust for the district. The congregation treats its property completely as its own unless there is division or the congregation is dissolved.

Brethren take seriously the statements of Jesus which lead to a shared leadership and a spirit of mutual helpfulness and service.

They also take seriously the New Testament teachings that we are not to be like a foot disconnected from the body or a hand which feels no responsibility to the arm. We are to be members of one another.

To do: Volunteer for some task at church where you have special gifts. It may be simple, like mowing the lawn or washing dishes, or more public, like assisting in teaching a Sunday School class or singing in the choir.

Some scriptures . . .

Jesus' view of religious lordship—Matthew 23
Each with a gift which belongs to all—1 Corinthians 12:4–30, Romans 12:6–8

Every member a minister—Ephesians 4:11–16

For further reading . . .

Dennis L. Slabaugh, "Annual Meeting," *The Brethren Encyclopedia*, Donald Durnbaugh, editor, 1983: volume 1, pp. 32–39.

Manual of Worship and Polity of the Church of the Brethren.

7

To Let Him Live in Us

Early American patriot and leader Benjamin Franklin tells in his *Autobiography* of his surprise at meeting young Michael Wohlfahrt. Franklin was under the impression that Wohlfahrt was Brethren. Franklin asks him, "What is your creed?" He is surprised to find that these Brethren do not have a creed. Franklin's *Autobiography* records that Wohlfahrt explained the position this way:

> When we were first drawn together as a society, it had pleased God to enlighten our minds so far as to see that some doctrines, which once we esteemed errors, were real truths. From time to time God has been pleased to afford us further light, and our principles have been improving and our errors diminishing.
>
> Now we are not sure that we have arrived at the end of this progression and at the perfection of spiritual or theological knowledge, and we fear that if we should once print our confession of faith we should feel ourselves as if bound or confined by it, and perhaps be unwilling to receive further improvement.

God is not finished with any of us yet. God has more to say to us than our little minds can even begin to understand. Jesus said this to his disciples after living with them for some time. "I have yet many things to say to you, but you cannot bear them now. When the Spirit of Truth comes, he will guide you into all truth" (John 16:12–13).

Our attachment is to Jesus: to let him take our lives, to trust him and go with him wherever he takes us, to let him live in us.

Openness and Honesty

Brethren believe that Jesus teaches honesty and openness. Of the early Brethren it was said, "Their word is as good as their bond." What they say is as good as a written contract. They tried to live Jesus' admonition to let what you say be simply "yes" or "no" (Matthew 5:37; James 5:12). The Brethren value open discussion and decision-making.

From the outset, they counselled against belonging to secret organizations such as lodges. The Christian does not live a hidden, shadowy life; we are to "walk in the light as He is in the light" (1 John 1:7; 2 Cor. 4:2).

To Believe in Christ Is to Go with Him

The story is told of a famous tightrope walker from France who visited the United States in the 1930s. He announced his intention to have a cable stretched across Niagara Falls and to push an assistant in a wheelbarrow across the Falls over that cable.

The morning came for his announced event. A crowd had gathered. The first winks of the morning sun were to be seen in the dark sky. Below was the pounding of the water on the rocks, and the air was filled with the cold mist from the spray.

The tightrope artist walked up to one person in the crowd. "Do you believe that I can do this?" he asked. "Yes, I believe that you can do it," the onlooker replied. "Good," said the artist. "The man who was to have been in the wheelbarrow didn't show up today. You will take his place."

To believe in Christ is not something we do with our minds alone. Believing involves our minds. But belief in the New Testament involves going with him, doing the things he asks, because we believe him to be the One Scripture says he is.

To follow Christ means that we come to the Bible with our hearts and minds open. We do not come with the idea already on our minds as to what following him means. We do not come seeking support for what we already believe and for what we already do. We come asking. We come seeking. We come as disciples—learners—wanting to know.

There is an old rabbinical story about the Polish National Pistol Champion who was touring Europe. He came across a barn on a farm where there were targets painted. At the very center of each bull's eye was a bullet hole.

The champion called to the farmer. "This is amazing marksmanship. Who did the shooting? From what distance?" The old farmer showed him the distance. "Amazing," said the champion. "It was done by an old rabbi," said the farmer.

The champion insisted on meeting the rabbi.

"You did the shooting?" asked the champion. "Yes," replied the rabbi. "And from that distance?" "Yes," replied the rabbi. "Well," said the rabbi as a smile came to his lips. "Actually I shoot first, and then I draw the circles."

Many Christians come to the Bible to read into it what they want to find there. The English writer Shakespeare said that even the devil can quote scripture for his purposes.

To take no creed but Christ is to come to Scripture asking to be taught. It is to come willing to let life and thinking be revised. It is to come seeking that our little minds will take on the very mind of Christ.

The Gospel Is Both Personal and Social

Christians have tended to divide into two groups.

Some Christians have stressed **personal salvation**. They talk of a personal Christ who brings salvation from sin and the promise of hope in time of suffering and death.

Other Christians have talked about **a social** gospel. They have been concerned about justice and peace.

Jesus did not use either term. Jesus did not talk about personal salvation or about a social gospel. For Jesus it was one gospel and one salvation and both were immediately both social and personal.

Because they grew out of a time of war and torture over religion, from the outset in 1708 the Brethren have been concerned about war and justice and so-called "social" issues.

Because they grew out of a time when there was great corruption among Christians—great immorality and personal sin even among religious leaders—from the beginning in 1708, the Brethren have been concerned about the personal message of the gospel.

Long ago the English poet Swinburne wrote: "For tender minds they served up half a Christ." Brethren are committed to the whole gospel.

In the traditional Brethren emblem—a seal probably originating with Alexander Mack, Jr.—is symbolized both concerns. Central is the cross on which is superimposed a heart, suggesting strong emphasis on sacrifice and devotion. The heart represents the personal aspect. But included is a vine laden with grapes representing the fruit of the gospel. The vine springs from the heart, symbolizing the fact that faith must result in lives that bear fruit of outward actions.

Jesus was very much concerned about individuals weighed down with personal sin. Adultery, stealing, selfishness, pride, and self-righteousness were all concerns that he raised.

But Jesus also walked into the temple to cleanse it of money changers who were using an unjust system to take from the very poor what they were not financially able to give.

Jesus followed in the tradition of the great Hebrew prophets who insisted that God wants not only love and devotion but righteousness—justice—toward all people.

At the very outset of his ministry, he announced that his aim was to proclaim release to the captives, recovery of sight to the blind, to set at liberty those who are oppressed, and to proclaim the year of the Lord's favor. (Luke 4:18–19)

Jesus takes up the concern of the earlier scriptures that God wants for his people justice and peace.

For Brethren, as they read Jesus, there is no such thing as sin that has no public consequence. In this sense, **there are no personal sins.** All sins have social implications. Immorality, intemperance, lying, little personal thefts, these all affect my home, my family, my neighbors, my job, my world.

The drinking driver is not engaging in a purely personal pastime. He affects all around him. On the highway he is a potential killer, a potential destroyer of life and happiness of people whom he does not even know.

Likewise, there are no sins that cannot be traced to personal actions. In this sense, **there are no social sins.** To call war a social sin is to make it impersonal and, therefore, an acceptable thing. War is sin because it destroys people. It burns homes, it cripples and kills children of God, it tears apart and destroys human beings.

Racial or religious hatred is not impersonal. People are involved both as the haters and the hated: mothers and fathers and little children who laugh and cry, who feel pain, who have hopes and needs just like you and me.

Nothing on this earth is entirely my own business. Every act of mine is like throwing a pebble into a pond; it sets up a widening circle of response which, in a sense, never ends.

And nothing on this earth is entirely social. Every social decision and action ultimately involves people.

Witness at the United Nations and in Washington, D.C.

Brethren realize that our faith also touches the secular human structures of which we are a part. We have had a witness in Washington, D.C., speaking to the US government, and at the United Nations. All of life must come under the love and judgment of God.

One Gospel

There is one gospel—the gospel of Jesus. It is as personal and as warm as the phrase from John 3:16: "God so loved . . . that he sent his son." And it is as broad and deep as the other part of that verse which reminds us that God so loved "the world," not just Christians, not just the church. But God loves all the world. God cares about every area of life, and we must, too.

So for Brethren, we must ask **one** question, "Where would you take us, Jesus? What do you want of us?"

And as answers come to us, if we love him, we will go with him. We will do what he asks.

To do: This week translate one belief into concrete action. Do not be only a "Bible believer." Act on one belief and become a "Bible doer."

Some scriptures . . .

Jesus did not come to bring a new religion but life—John 10:10
What God really wants—Micah 6:6–8
Songs of praise are not enough—Amos 5:18–24
Not everyone who says "Lord, Lord"—Matthew 7:15–23
The greatest commandment—Matthew 22:35–40
The weightier matters of the law—Matthew 23:23
Parting words at the Last Supper—John 15:12–17
The tests of love—1 John 3:17–18; 1 John 4:19–21
"Work is love made visible"—James 2:14–17

8

All War Is Sin

The Church of the Brethren has been called one of the "historic peace churches" —along with the Quakers and the Mennonites.

Actually the first "historic peace church" was the church of the New Testament.

For the first three hundred years we have no evidence that Christians went to war. The early church was an outlaw religion in the Roman empire. Christians would not bow down and worship the Roman emperor. And Christians refused to serve in the army.

They suffered persecution and death for this refusal. But the more they were persecuted, the more they grew. As one early church historian observed, "The blood of the martyrs was the seed of the church." As they willingly died for their faith, the church grew in dedication and spiritual strength and in numbers.

All that changed when the Emperor Constantine, in 313, became a Christian. The nature of the church changed at that point. From a position of persecution it came to have a position of favor. Where there had been wide-ranging debates over creeds before, now church councils were called to reconcile differences, and those who disagreed with decisions came to be branded as heretics and were driven out.

Whereas Christians had not gone to war before Constantine, the emperor had his armies baptized. Constantine heard words from God. He said: "By **this** sign conquer."

In his dream he saw a sign of the cross. Rather than taking **the way** of the cross, he had a cross painted on the shield of each soldier.

Although earlier Christians had not gone to war, the time came when no one could serve in the Roman army unless he was a Christian.

Growing out of a period of thirty years of war between Christians and driven back to the Scriptures for answers, the early Brethren discovered again the position of the early church and studied the Scriptures to try to discover why the early church had been so insistent against all war and violence.

Old Testament Foundations

The message of peace begins with the very first verses of Old Testament scripture. The creation stories tell of the importance of people in God's plan. They are created in God's own image and are to have a special relationship to God (Gen. 1:27).

When Cain murders his brother Abel, God places a mark on Cain's forehead, not as a curse but as a protection. No one is to kill Cain (Gen. 4:1–16). It is the beginning of the gospel which the Apostle Paul will stress much later, "Vengeance is mine, I will repay, says the Lord" (Rom. 12:19). The taking of human life belongs to God.

They saw the struggles of the Hebrew people. On the one hand, the Hebrews attempt to secure God's blessings for their wars and killing. But the other message kept coming through in passages like Psalm 8 which says that people are made a little lower than God and the message of Zechariah 4:6: "Not by might nor by power but by my spirit, says the Lord of hosts."

They read of King David and his wars (believing he has God's blessing!), but they also read of David's desire to build a temple to God and of God's rebuke of David, telling the king that he was unworthy to build the temple because of the blood of warfare on his hands (1 Kings 5:3; 1 Chronicles 28:2–3).

They read the popular folk beliefs of the people that it was God who urged them on, to kill every living thing as they took enemy cities, to slaughter even the babies of those they hated (Psalm 137:9).

But Brethren, like many other Christians, came to see that the Bible is the story of **God's unfolding revelation**. It is the story of the growing understanding of men and women of God. And it is the story of a God who only bit by bit breaks through the hardness of our hearts and the dullness of our minds.

They read the harsh words of some Old Testament leaders. But they had to place alongside these the majestic views of some of the lonely prophets who in their own day were sometimes overlooked or called traitors (Jer. 26).

Jeremiah's plea for peace was unmistakable. Isaiah's vision of the future was grand indeed (Isa. 9:5–7). The outline of a time when people will "beat their swords into plowshares and their spears into pruning hooks and not learn war any more" could not be ignored (Isa. 2:2–4).

Even the simple story of Jonah flew in the face of the logic of that day (Jonah 4:10–11). God was bigger than the smallness of their minds.

Jesus: the Prince of Peace

But for Brethren, the heart of the message came from Jesus himself. Jesus was the Word made flesh. (John 1:14) Jesus was the highest, holiest, most perfect revelation. (Hebrews 1:1–3) And everything else had to be read in the light of his life, his teachings, and his death and resurrection, if Jesus was indeed the Christ.

David was not the Messiah. Moses was not the Messiah. Jesus is the Messiah. He must be our creed, our ultimate rule for faith and practice.

The early Brethren looked carefully at the difficult scriptures. Jesus talked of bringing division (or a "sword") between father and son, mother and daughter (Matt. 10:34–39 and Luke 12:49–53).

But clearly in the context this was not an excuse for the mass killing of war. It was talking about the very real misunderstandings that will come toward all who seriously follow Christ.

Jesus had warned of difficult times to come. He urged his disciples to buy a sword (Luke 22:36). But again, in context, it was clear this was not meant for war. He was simply warning of difficult times ahead.

In the garden of Gethsemane as soldiers came to arrest Jesus, the disciples would gladly have taken up the cause. Peter took a sword and sliced off the ear of the slave of the High Priest.

Jesus healed the ear and turned to Simon Peter and said to him "Put away your sword. All who take the sword will perish by the sword" (Matt. 26:51–52).

They looked at the cleansing of the temple in John 2:13–18. A surface reading finds violence against people there. But the Greek makes clear that he overturned the tables of the money-changers and took a whip of cords and began to drive out the animals, not people (John 2:15).

In a day when hated Roman soldiers of occupation were everywhere, when they could and did abuse Jesus' people, Jesus was able to look past the uniform and deal with them as persons. On one occasion he said, "Never in all Israel have I found such faith" as he found in a Roman officer who came to him (Matt. 8:10).

He told his people that if they were compelled to carry a soldier's pack a mile, as by law they could be, they were to carry it two miles. If compelled to yield over their outer garment, they were to give their jacket as well. If slapped, they were to turn the other cheek (Matt. 5:38–48).

It was a strange new way of dealing with meanness. Jesus' followers in the first century did not understand it any better than we do.

The Heart of the Message: the Cross

But the strongest impact came not from the life or teachings of Jesus, all of which moved toward a love which never stoops to the adversary's level.

The strongest impact came from the very heart of the gospel—the cross.

Jesus, who had the power to resist, instead let them nail him to a cross and crucify him.

Even as he was dying, he looked down in his pain at his tormentors and killers and said, "Father, forgive them. They do not know what they are doing" (Luke 23:34).

Jesus was a totally different kind of leader. Rather than winning, he lost— everything. But in that loss he proved the power and love of God. As Paul was to write, the cross seems folly to the world (1 Cor. 1:20–30).

Easter Sunday morning was the bold evidence that life is stronger than death, that love is stronger than hate, that light is stronger than the powers of darkness, that good can indeed overcome evil in God's good time (Rom. 12:14–21).

Freedom to Find Our Way

The Brethren have rejected war as a way to solve differences between people because they are serious about living the way Jesus asks.

At the same time, Brethren know that it is difficult to have a clear witness when the nations in which we live are caught up in war systems. Brethren are committed even here to encouraging each member to follow his or her own conscience.

During World War II, many Brethren in the United States served in the armed forces. Others served in **Civilian Public Service Camps** as an alternative to military service—doing work of national importance in prisons or mental hospitals, fighting forest fires, or letting their bodies be used as human "guinea pigs" for medical experiments. Some were in starvation units to assist medical science in discovering ways to bring people back from the brink of starvation.

A few Brethren have believed that conscription for military service is wrong, that the draft system itself is evil, and have refused even to register for the draft. Some of these have gone to prison for their convictions.

Some Examples

There have been examples of great heroism and sacrifice because of this desire to take Jesus very seriously in this difficult area.

A popular story among Brethren says that one of the early leaders, **John Naas**, as a young man was a head taller than most of his friends. Because of his strong body, he was stopped by soldiers of the King of Prussia who tried to enlist him in the king's personal bodyguard. Naas refused.

The soldiers tied young Naas up by his left thumb and his right big toe. Still he refused.

Taking him before the king, the king himself questioned the young man. "Why do you refuse?" the king asked.

Naas replied, "Sir, I cannot and will not serve in your guard. Long ago I enlisted in another army. I will not be a traitor to my king."

"Who is your king?" the ruler asked. "My king," said Naas, "is the Prince Immanuel, our Lord Jesus Christ. I have chosen his way. I cannot and will not forsake him."

The king was moved by the lad's dedication. "Neither will I ask you to forsake him," he said, and he gave John Naas a gold coin as he dismissed him.

Christopher Sauer I, an early American printer, a business rival of Benjamin Franklin, was a friend of the Brethren. He printed the first foreign language Bibles in the United States and circulated a newspaper among German-speaking immigrants.

Over the door of his shop was a motto, "To the glory of God and my neighbor's Good."

Christopher Sauer II, an elder in the church, refused to take an oath of loyalty to the revolutionary government. He believed that war was wrong.

As a result, he was imprisoned. All of his extensive property (including houses, workshops, furnishings, and press) was confiscated and auctioned off, and he died a poor man.

In the early frontier days in America, Brethren refused to relate to the American Indian with violence and abuse. They went to live among the Indians unarmed, trying to treat them fairly and with kindness.

In the cove area in Blair County near Martinsburg, Pennsylvania, some of the Indians did not understand that these white people were different. There was a massacre of the unarmed Brethren that lived there. (The Indians of Morrison's Cove were impressed by the behavior of the Brethren and asked decades later about them.)

Sometimes their faith has meant suffering and death. But they have not wavered from their desire to be faithful to the understanding shared by the Christ.

During Nigeria's civil war from 1967 to 1969, members of the church in Nigeria and in the United States joined hands to give valuable relief service of medicine, food distribution, agriculture, and administration during and after the conflict.

Some of their relief went to Biafrans who were considered the Nigerians' enemies.

During and since World War II, the United States government has granted **conscientious objectors** to war the opportunity for alternative service to military service in areas which are designated as being of national importance.

During the Vietnam War, a young Brethren volunteer, Ted Studebaker, was living in a Vietnamese village and working with other Christian volunteers to help Vietnamese during the fighting to dig wells and improve farming.

One night, a week after he had been married, he was killed by a group of wandering Vietnamese who killed and looted.

Ted Studebaker was in an area where no American GI was permitted to go alone. He was serving unarmed and unafraid.

John Barwick was a Brethren who worked for the YMCA in Arab refugee camps. He moved through those camps unarmed and unafraid, going places where most Americans would have been killed on sight.

Peace: a Message the World Needs Now

With the terrible weapons that have been developed and the possibility of destroying the planet earth, many thoughtful people are now convinced that war is irrational and wrong.

Brethren came to that decision long ago because they discovered the early church for three hundred years had believed that was what Jesus taught. And as the early Brethren read and studied Jesus, they too felt that this was what he taught. Because they were committed to living Christ's way, they have been willing to risk the cost involved.

G. K. Chesterton once said, "Jesus has never been tried and found wanting. Jesus has been found difficult and seldom tried."

To do: This week help mend one fight or area of brokenness. Be a peacemaker at least once.

Some scriptures . . .

God is the author of peace—Luke 2:13–14
Jesus is the prince of peace—Isaiah 9:5–7
Christians shall live in peace with all—Matthew 26:52; Romans 14:19; Mark 9:50
The Christian's method of resolving differences—Matthew 18:15–17
Forgiveness is essential to worshipping God—Matthew 5:23–24
The Christian's reluctance to go to civil court—1 Corinthians 6:1–6
The Christian response to evil—Matthew 5:43–48; Romans 12:19–21

For further reading . . .

Biblical Basis of a Peace Witness, Brethren Press, Elgin, Illinois.

D. W. Kurtz, *Ideals of the Church of the Brethren*, Brethren Press, Elgin, Illinois.

Dale H. Aukerman, "Conscientious Objection," *The Brethren Encyclopedia*, pp. 335–337, vol. 1.

9

The Cup of Cold Water

For Brethren, the message of Jesus is more than saying "No" to war. It is saying "Yes" to peacemaking.

The words in Jesus' story of the King at the Last Judgment, "Inasmuch as you have done it unto one of the least of these, you have done it unto me," have had great influence on our church (Matt. 25:35–36).

Since earliest days, the Brethren, though stripped of their riches because of their faith, shared what they had with others less fortunate.

During the War Between the States, John Kline ministered to both north and south.

Between the two world wars, Brethren sent aid to help the Armenians and Syrians and to both sides in the Spanish Civil War.

Serving "both sides" became the pattern for the Brethren. In 1939 the **Brethren Service Commission** was formed. It developed a program of service and rehabilitation across Europe and the Middle East.

At the end of World War II the Brethren had warehouses full of food and clothing ready to be shipped to their former enemies, the Germans.

Brethren Volunteer Service was formed. BVS makes possible the service by youth and adults around the world in tension spots where there is hatred or suffering.

Brethren have worked on the island of Cyprus to bring long-time enemies—Greek and Turkish Cypriots—together.

Brethren have sent youth behind the Iron Curtain to teach English and agriculture in Poland. They have brought Polish farmers to the United States.

Brethren have established ties with a pentecostal church in Cuba to bridge the barriers of hurt.

Brethren young people worked along the borders of El Salvador, helping fleeing refugees. **Yvonne Dilling** and other Brethren volunteers tried to provide a human shield of nonviolent love with their bodies against the violence in Central America.

Giving and Receiving in Councils of Churches

The Brethren have seen their mission not only to the non-Christian world around them but to other Christians as well. They have felt a special calling to re-introduce the gospel of peace to other denominations which may have forgotten it.

Brethren were actively involved in the formation of the World Council of Churches and of the National Council of Churches of Christ in the United States. They are actively involved in local and state Councils of Churches. Many Brethren have served as executives of such councils.

Brethren have had representatives to various evangelical associations and groups because they want to learn and to share about the full meaning of the gospel.

Their worldwide service effort, Brethren Service, was expanded to draw in as many other Christian groups as possible. The Brethren Service Center at New Windsor, Maryland, became a center for the newly formed Church World Service, with Brethren inviting others in to form a much larger agency which would belong to all Christians who would join.

During the Spanish Civil War, a young Brethren Indiana farmer, **Dan West**, was attempting to administer relief to both sides. One day while resting under a tree, he suddenly realized that a cow's milk is like the love of God. God makes the sun to shine on bad and good people alike, and gives rain to the evil and good (Matt. 5:45). A cow does not stop to ask if a person is Catholic or Protestant, democratic or fascist. A cow does not deny a hungry child because that child has the wrong parents. Dan West got the idea of Heifers for Relief, of sending a young cow bearing offspring with the provision that when the calf was born, it would be given to someone else. The project expanded to include dairy goats, sheep, pigs, chickens, rabbits, and bees as well as dairy and beef cattle. Again, what Brethren began and developed, they did not keep for themselves. Today, **Heifer Project International** is truly inter-denominational, involving many religious groups and individuals.

Between 1944 and 1979, Heifer Project provided livestock and poultry to 150 countries in Latin America and the Caribbean, in Asia, Africa, and the United States, without regard to race, creed, or political origin, and according to a plan which requires the one receiving to share the increase with others.

In the harshest days of the Cold War immediately following World War II, some of the first Americans to be admitted to the Soviet Union were a group of Brethren farmers who brought heifers to a Moscow orphanage.

CROP, the hunger appeal unit of Church World Service today, began as Christian Rural Overseas Program, again with Brethren leadership. The list goes on.

At New Windsor, Maryland, our church maintains a warehouse the size of a football field. The Brethren facilitate the receiving, warehousing, and shipping of medicines, medical supplies, and medical equipment on behalf of Interchurch Medical Assistance, Inc. IMA represents 18 denominations and agencies. Its purpose is to receive donated materials from various manufacturers and make them available to approximately 600 clinics and hospitals in more than 40 countries. IMA ships over $10 million worth of supplies each year.

SERRV Self-Help Crafts

The Brethren have developed a self-help program entitled SERRV Self-Help Crafts. Fine handcrafted items are made by crafts people from developing nations. The items are sent to the Brethren Service Center at New Windsor, Maryland, and distributed for sale to a growing network of SERRV giftshops throughout the United States. The money earned is returned to the crafts persons in their native land to support themselves and their families.

On Earth Peace

M. R. (Bob) Zigler was one of the key motivating forces behind the development of Brethren Service following World War II. In 1974, when he was in his mid-80s, Bob Zigler led in the establishment of "On Earth Peace," an effort to provide ongoing education and emphasis on peace, especially among Brethren. The program is centered in the Brethren Service Center in New Windsor, Maryland. Included is a Brethren World Peace Academy with conferences for high school and college age youth, held the first weekend of every month. Occasionally these Academies are held in various parts of the United States. An On Earth Peace Assembly is held periodically. The Assembly has sponsored the publication of books on peacemaking. A Brethren World Peace Bookstore is maintained at New Windsor as well. It serves churches and individuals in person and by mail.

Association of Brethren Caregivers

The Brethren have formed an **Association of Brethren Caregivers** which invites membership from all who are interested in health care ministries. They stand ready to assist congregations and communities in developing health ministries. One model is the Lafiya program already in operation in Nigeria, and they are beginning to share that model with Church of the Brethren congregations in communities throughout the United States and Puerto Rico.

For Brethren, the sharing of a "cup of cold water" in the name of Christ is basic (Matt. 10:42). And they have tried to reintroduce this essential part of the gospel wherever other Christians will join with them.

Heroes/Heroines

This pattern of service at home and in other nations has produced more than its share of heroes and heroines. We mention just five.

Miami Valor

Bill Bosler was pastor in Miami, Florida's First Church of the Brethren. He went about his work largely unnoticed by our denomination or by the city where he worked. He served in a racially troubled neighborhood. Under his leadership, the Miami congregation grew from 12 to 70: Salvadorans, Haitians, Puerto Ricans, Jamaicans, whites, American blacks and others. The poor, the alienated, the struggling, the young were among those he served.

Bill Bosler died the way he lived: reaching out to a young stranger in a poor, high-crime area filled with violence and danger. At 2 p.m., on December 22, 1986, he was murdered at the parsonage by someone who came to his home asking for help. He died with love toward the young man who attacked him.

Like Father/Like Daughter

SueZann Bosler, Bill Bosler's daughter, walked into the room where her father lay dying from knife wounds. His killer turned on SueZann, slashing her three times in the back and twice on her skull. Pretending to be dead, her life was spared. When the man left, she called for help.

It took months for SueZann to recover from the physical and emotional trauma she had suffered. Her lifelong opposition to the death penalty was put to the strongest possible test. Her father's convictions about the sacredness of life helped sustain her during that time. Several Bible passages strengthened her view that "only God has the right to take a human life."

The intruder, James Bernard Campbell, was arrested and convicted. The judge sentenced him to die in the electric chair. SueZann went to the judge to plead that the killer's life be spared. Since that time she has become an outspoken opponent of the death penalty, telling her story and appealing as a witness to the way of Christ, a way that advocates mercy in place of vengeance. "I want to give James Campbell something," she told Annual Conference in an emotional appearance. "I want him to have a Bible."

Global Servant

Lamar Gibble, as staff person for the denomination, is better known in the world's most volatile areas, such as sections of the Middle East or Northern Ireland, than in his own denomination. He quietly and consistently goes about the task of world peacemaking. Whether it is in writing a World Council of Churches resolution on disarmament or leading a delegation to the German Democratic Republic, he expresses the Church of the Brethren witness as it is simultaneously translated into German,

French, Russian, Polish, Spanish, and other languages. Always the message is the same: strong support for a peaceful resolution of conflict. In 1987, Lamar received the highest civilian award of the Polish government, the Gold Medal of the Order of Merit of the Polish People's Republic, on the 30th anniversary of the Church of the Brethren's exchange program with Polish farmers. The exchange was begun at a time when Cold War tensions ran high. The award was Poland's highest medal of state for citizens of other countries. On receiving the award, Lamar said, "The award was not to honor me but to honor the program."

Death Row Angel

Wanda Callahan was pastor of the Church of the Brethren in Jacksonville, Florida. In 1975, Kenneth Charles Foster and three others killed a salesman in a drunken brawl in a Florida tavern. Wanda Callahan had a ministry to prisoners on death row in Jacksonville State Prison where Kenneth Foster awaited execution. Through her ministry, Kenny Foster became a Christian and was baptized into the Church of the Brethren.

On October 16, 1984, Kenneth Foster was scheduled to be executed by the State of Florida. He asked Pastor Wanda to stay with him during the last hours and then act as a witness during the execution. It is important for the condemned person to have eye contact with someone who, they know, has a genuine concern for them while they are being strapped into the chair, before the hood is placed over their head.

Late the night before, something unbelievable happened. Suddenly doors opened that before had been closed. The judge allowed witnesses and reports to be submitted that had never been allowed in all nine years. The others who were party to the killing had been given their freedom in exchange for their testimony against Foster. There would be a stay of execution for Foster.

The lawyer and his staff were dumbfounded. But Pastor Wanda Callahan called it a miracle.

Knowing that he would not be put to death, Kenny's brothers and sisters wanted to make a confession to Christ. They prayed, talked, confessed, and cried for an hour. They sang "Happy Birthday" to Kenny Foster. All this happened because of the unrelenting caring of one amazing pastor who reached out in time of need to a person for whom nobody else cared.

Korean Convert

Dan (Kwang Suk) Kim was the first Korean Church of the Brethren pastor. As a Korean youth in a land where military service is demanded of all young men, he chose the chaplaincy. Even so, to the great embarrassment of his superiors, he refused to sign the expected loyalty oath to the repressive Korean government and its harsh dictator, Park Chung Hee. He turned the paper over and wrote "no."

Dan says, his superior "turned yellow" with fright. So Dan took his "no" vote to the officer over them. The officer took one look and in anger tore up the paper. Dan could have been sent to prison.

As a young man, for three years Dan worked among rag pickers in Korea, the poorest of Korea's poor. They did not trust him until one of them needed an operation. Dan arranged this and was the only one willing to give blood for the man. After that, the rag pickers gave him their confidence. Dan chose the Church of the Brethren because he had long searched for that kind of church. As a boy he had been a Buddhist. As a Christian for a long time he had tried to do whatever Jesus asks. In the Brethren, he found such a fellowship of Christians.

For Brethren, service at home or around the world is basic to being Christian. They seek to pattern their lives after the Christ they love who said, "I am among you as one who serves."

To do: This week find a need and meet it. Find some hurt and heal it.

Some scriptures . . .

God is the author of peace—Luke 2:13–14
Jesus is the prince of peace—Isaiah 9:6–7
Christians shall live in peace with all—Matthew 26:52; Romans 14:19; Mark 9:50
The Christian's method of resolving differences—Matthew 18:15–17
Forgiveness is essential to worshipping God—Matthew 5:23–24
The Christian's reluctance to go to civil court—1 Corinthians 6:1–6
The Christian response to evil—Matthew 5:43–48; Romans 12:19–21

For further reading . . .

Biblical Basis of a Peace Witness, The Brethren Press, Elgin, Illinois.

D. W. Kurtz, *Ideals of the Church of the Brethren,* The Brethren Press, Elgin, Illinois.

J. Kenneth Kreider, "Brethren Service Commission," *The Brethren Encyclopedia,* Donald F. Durnbaugh editor, 1983: pp. 198-201, vol. 1.

John D. Metzler, Sr., "Christian Rural Overseas Program," *The Brethren Encyclopedia,* pp. 286-287, vol. 1.

Dale H. Aukerman, "Conscientious Objection," *The Brethren Encyclopedia,* pp. 335-337, vol. 1

Thurl Metzger, "Heifer Project International," *The Brethren Encyclopedia,* pp. 593-594, vol. 1.

10

Of One Blood

One of the moving stories in the book of Acts is of Simon Peter, a respected leader in the church, bold and strong and wise, but a deeply racially prejudiced person as well.

Acts 10 tells of Peter, asleep on the roof of a home, dreaming that God has let down on a sheet all kinds of food for him to eat. Three times God invited Peter to rise and eat. But on that sheet are foods which the Jews considered unclean. Three times Peter refuses, saying that he has never eaten anything that is common or unclean. And three times God tells Peter, "What God has cleansed you must not call unclean."

As Peter wakes and reflects on what this might mean, he is confronted with men sent by Cornelius, a Roman centurion, who wants Peter to come to his home.

A good Jew would never go to a Gentile home, stay there, eat the food of such people, and have fellowship with them.

But Peter, remembering the dream, goes and shares his faith with a non-Jew. At the end of that experience, Cornelius and his family ask to be baptized.

The request goes against all that Peter has believed and practiced all his life. With his earliest training he received the notion that Jews are God's special people. All others are "gentiles," which simply means "the nations." Everyone else was common or unclean.

The Apostle Paul had been going across the known world to plant Christian churches among the gentiles.

Paul believed that "in Christ Jesus there is neither Jew nor Greek, neither slave nor free, neither male nor female" (Gal. 3:28). Paul believed that God had made of one blood every nation to live on all the face of the earth (Acts 17:26).

But Peter had trouble accepting that. Peter had been at the forefront of the leadership which demanded that Paul give some explanation for his actions (Gal. 2:11–14; Acts 15).

But now, in this moment, mature Peter experienced yet another conversion—another "turning"—in his life. He said, "I now realize that it is true that God treats everyone on the same basis. Whoever fears him and does what is right is acceptable to him, no matter what race he belongs to" (Acts 10:34).

One of the messages which Brethren have drawn from the Scriptures is at this very point. They have insisted that God's favor is not determined by the color of the skin or the language or the tribe or class.

Some Examples of Courage

John Kline was moderator of Annual Conference during America's Civil War over slavery.

John Kline lived in Virginia—in the south. But Kline, like the other Brethren did not believe in holding slaves.

Indeed, some blacks were members of the Church of the Brethren even in the south at that time.

Although he opposed slavery, John Kline also believed war was wrong. During the war, as moderator of the entire church, he would ride across the battle lines into the north to preach. Sometimes he would return late at night on his good horse, Nell.

One day as John Kline was returning home, as he was riding into his lane, he was shot from ambush and killed.

Some have suggested that John Kline must have been killed by strangers who did not know him because he was such a good man. But neighbors in that Virginia community say that he was killed by neighbors who knew him very well but could not understand or tolerate a man who loved all people—black and white, north and south.

During the civil rights struggle in the 1960s in the United States, a white student at Manchester College, one of the denomination's six colleges, decided that he wanted to study a year at Fisk University, a black school of higher education.

During the first weeks there Paul LePrad, the Brethren student, was quiet, almost unnoticed. He went about his studies and stayed pretty much to himself.

In the South at that time black people were not served at lunch counters designated for whites. A handful of black students at Fisk went to a local drugstore lunch counter and sat there waiting to be served. They were so poor that if they had been served they might not have had money to pay for it. They were largely ignored.

One Saturday, as the handful of blacks sat at the counter, Paul LePrad showed up and went to the counter and sat with them.

The whites in the drugstore were furious. They began to swear at LePrad and call him names.

Paul said nothing. He simply sat there with his hands folded on the counter. This made them even more angry. One man held a burning cigarette against the back of LePrad's neck.

Still he said nothing, made no response, only sat there.

Some of the people pulled Paul LePrad from his lunch counter stool and began to beat and kick him.

A *Newsweek* magazine photographer was there and took a series of photographs. Those photographs went around the world.

The president of Fisk University told Earl Garver, the dean of Manchester College, that up until that time the sit-in efforts in the South had been largely unsuccessful. Tiny groups of students had gone without widespread support.

But at that point things changed. The fact that a white student would voluntarily go and sit with them and take upon himself the hatred and violence meant for them suddenly aroused them. Suddenly black students began to turn out in large numbers. The sit-in movement caught on across the south.

Isaiah 53 talks of the Suffering Servant bearing our grief and carrying our sorrows. It says that all our sins are laid at last on him. Christians see Jesus in that passage. They see the cross.

There is a term in Christian theology, **"vicarious suffering,"** the willingness of people to take another's sorrow and pain and slavery on themselves. Across Christian history is the frail line of stories of those who have given of themselves freely—**"the everlasting wounds that heal the world."**

The concern for peace among God's people of which we spoke is more than passive submission to evil. At times it has come through with great strength, like moral judo, appealing to the good that is present even in the midst of great evil, using the opponents' own goodness to call forth a better way of living.

In Selma, Alabama, after a massive civil rights march, that community in the deep South was torn apart by hatred and mistrust. Brethren peacemaker **Ralph Smeltzer** went and lived in that community following the march to quietly bring together voices of reason and goodness, white and black, that people could live together once again.

The vision of our Lord is clear. The Great Commission commands the disciples to start in their own hometowns. But the gospel they have been granted is **for all the world,** "for every group, every tribe, every people" (Matt. 28:19; Luke 24:47).

Brethren came to the United States as German farmers. Gradually they went beyond the German language barrier and began to reach others. They settled first in the farmlands of Pennsylvania, Virginia, Ohio, Indiana, Illinois, and Iowa, then on to the farms of Washington, Oregon, and California.

They then went to the cities. And now they have broken other ethnic barriers. There has been special emphasis on work among blacks, Hispanics, Koreans, Kampucheans, Chinese, and other peoples and cultures. Mission work took them to Denmark, China, India, Nigeria, Ecuador, and Indonesia.

When **H. Stover Kulp** went to Nigeria in 1922, he was concerned about establishing churches and medical facilities and schools and agricultural improvement. But one of the first things he did was to create a written system for the Bura and Marghi languages and then to translate parts of the Bible and educational materials. He wanted the people he served to receive the faith in their own "heart language." The Christian faith would not be a foreign religion but would be their very own.

As various language groups have come into the church in the United States, they have spilled back to the country of those other language immigrants.

The Church of the Brethren is becoming a world church for all people, respecting the distinctiveness of every culture but with no barriers of love toward people, whatever their racial background.

That is the way they believe their Lord would want it.

To do: Learn to know someone of another race or culture. Learn how life seems to them.

Some scriptures . . .

Of one blood—Acts 17:26

God shows no partiality—Acts 10:34

The early church was interracial (Simon who carried the cross was thought to have been black; his two sons were members of the early church)—Matthew 27:32; Mark 15:21; Romans 16:13

God loves all peoples—Amos 9:7

In Christ Jesus we are all one—Galatians 3:28; Ephesians 2:13–18; Colossians 3:11

A house of prayer for all peoples—Isaiah 56:7

11

Stewards of God's Good Gifts

"You are not your own; you were bought with a price," the Apostle Paul wrote (1 Cor. 6:19–20). So great is God's sacrificial investment in us, we know that we are loved (1 John 3:1–3; Rom. 8:12–17).

People are God's most important creation (Gen. 1:28; Psalm 8:6–8). That's why war is so terribly wrong. That is why racial prejudice is so evil. War and racial prejudice destroy and hurt people.

And **you** are important to God. You are one of those people that God cares for.

The Simple Life

Brethren have talked of the "**simple life**." They have been concerned about materialism and focus on money. Too many "things" can blind our eyes to human values. Too much wealth can keep us from each other.

Jesus said to the rich young ruler, "Sell everything and give the money to the poor and come, follow me" (Matt. 19:21). He said, "You cannot serve God and money" (Matt. 6:24). He told of the poor man, Lazarus, who sat at the gate of the rich man and begged for crumbs. The rich man ignored him. But when they both died, the rich man was in hell and the poor man was in the bosom of Abraham (Luke 16:19–31).

Jesus said, "It is more difficult for a rich man to enter the kingdom of heaven than for a camel to pass through the eye of a needle" (Matt. 19:24).

It is like a window and silver. Put too much silver on that window and you have only a mirror. Instead of being able to look through that glass and see others, we see only ourselves.

We need always to make certain that we use "things" and that "things" do not consume, control, and use us. You are more important than clothes, Jesus said. You are more important than the physical things you may fret and worry over (Matt. 6:24–34).

The early Brethren lived in a time of pretense and extravagance. Many people of that day were consumed with trying to impress others. Many would rarely bathe and then cover over the body odors with heavy perfumes. Some had lice in their hair and wore wigs. They dressed for show.

People were very aware of status. If someone visited a prince, how he or she was seated depended upon their rank in society. An equal would sit on a chair on the rug on which the prince sat. A lower rank might sit with two legs of the chair on the same rug. Someone still lower would sit off the rug or stand. This was not the way the Brethren understood that God would want people to relate to one another.

Titles and degrees interfered with understanding and relationships. Brethren came to address one another as "brother" or "sister" or by their first names. Across the years Brethren have shied away from using terms like "doctor" when addressing others.

In terms of material possessions, they tried to stay a step or two **behind** their neighbors, rather than scratching frantically to keep up with the passion to impress each other. Humility and genuineness were important virtues.

When extravagant dress was so important to society, they consciously chose to wear the garb of the peasant class. As styles changed, this simple way of dressing became known as "the plain clothes." Mennonites and Quakers also chose to dress this way.

Most Brethren no longer wear plain clothes, but they still are concerned about simplicity. They strive for a life which is more concerned about faithfulness to God and about the welfare of people than about outer trimmings.

The Stewardship of Money

The Old Testament made clear that a **tithe** of all we earn—one-tenth—belongs to God. The very last book of the Old Testament, Malachi, talks of people cheating God. The challenge is issued to bring "the full tithe" to the Temple and put God to the test to see if God in turn will not open the windows of heaven and pour out on us abundance of all kinds of good things (Mal. 3:8–10). Jesus said of the tithe: "This you **ought** to have done" (Matt. 23:23).

Brethren have believed we must take our stewardship to God seriously. We should not let the freedom of Christ mean that we do less toward God than the poorest Jew did. We need to give, not for God's sake or for the church's sake but for **our** sakes.

Because we have been given much, we in turn need to express our thanks in ways that are significant enough that our lives are pulled into line with God's purposes. To give too little, to refuse to acknowledge how important God is to us, is to live life without purpose. It is as we let the claims of God's kingdom take control of our lives that everything else falls into proper perspective (Matt. 6:33).

The Stewardship of All the Earth

Brethren believe the stewardship of the other nine-tenths of what we earn must be used wisely and well also. The very word **steward** originally referred to a keeper of pigs, a sty ward, the overseer of a pig sty. "The earth is the Lord's" (Psalm 24:1). The entire world belongs to God. So the preservation of the earth is important. While any of God's children are hungry, we dare not hoard. If some have more than they need while others have less than they need, we must be concerned (Luke 3:11).

The Stewardship of Families

Family life has been important to Brethren, strong homes where children are raised in love and with the security of two parents whose presence and support will never be questioned (Matt. 19:1–9). Broken homes mean broken lives.

The commitment made in marriage is for life and is to be regarded as sacred. Because people matter, the pressures of sin which would destroy homes must be faced.

The Apostle Paul, as he dealt with immorality and evil in his day, told early Christians, "You are God's temple. That temple must not be dirtied and soiled. It must be kept clean if it is to be the dwelling place for the most holy God (1 Cor. 3:16–17).

The Stewardship of Our Own Bodies

Because Brethren care about people, they are concerned about the ways in which human beings destroy **themselves** as well as about the ways in which they destroy others.

The Brethren have never felt comfortable with the word *temperance*. Temperance implies moderation. The Greeks preached moderation in all things.

Jesus took a stronger view. Jesus said that if something will lead to our downfall, tear it away and cast it off. Life is too precious to entertain things which destroy. (Matthew 18:6–9)

For Brethren, the phrase that had meaning to them and seemed to best capture the spirit of their Lord was "**Moderation in things good, abstinence (saying 'no') in things that are harmful.**"

Food is good. But too much food can kill. People can dig their graves with their teeth.

Work is good. But people can work too long, too hard.

In our world there are many areas where good things can be used in the wrong and harmful way.

Metal may be used for a scalpel by a surgeon to bring healing, or metal may be used for a switchblade or shrapnel to hurt. Wood may be used to build homes, or wood may be fashioned into a cross on which to crucify the Son of God.

When I was a very small child, I discovered a box of watercolors. In those days watercolors were not childproof. They were poisonous. They were so bright and pretty that I started to eat them like candy. My parents tell me that I almost died.

That does not mean that watercolors are sinful. It simply means that watercolors are not meant to be eaten.

Tobacco has many good uses in our world. Tobacco is used to delouse chickens. Some have found that ground tobacco leaves are good mulch for starting new lawns.

But medical science knows that when it is smoked, **tobacco kills**. It causes serious health problems. And for many it may lead to death. Smoking can cause cancer and breathing problems, results that dehumanize and hurt God's most precious creation, people. Smoking affects the health of everyone around the one who smokes.

Alcohol has many industrial and household uses. But medical science knows that in the human system, **alcohol kills.**

It affects judgment. It strips away the layers which civilization has been placing around us for centuries to make us truly human. First, it affects moral judgment and then mental and physical judgment.

The pain to which it contributes is impressive.

Estimates are that one-third of all suicides are alcohol-related. Half of all rapes and violent crimes are alcohol-related.

Half of all highway accidents in the United States are alcohol-related and 90 percent of all fatal highway accidents are alcohol-related. Often the fatal accidents do not involve drunkenness so much as they involve people with a few drinks who are unable to respond quickly enough to avoid disaster.

More Americans were killed on the highways of the United States in alcohol-related accidents than were killed in Vietnam during that war.

The estimates from medical people are that one person in twelve who drinks becomes an alcoholic. Their lives become unmanageable and they are unable to control their thirst for alcohol. The end result of alcoholism is death.

No one sets out to be an alcoholic. Those who drink believe that they can control it. Yet one in twelve has life destroyed and one in four who drinks has serious problems because of it.

Alcohol attacks every organ in the body. Alcohol in any amount destroys brain cells which are never replaced. Drinking over time results in "induced senility." Brethren believe that "it is a terrible thing to waste a mind."

Brethren have raised several questions. What is my responsibility to myself and my own life as I look at the ways that harm can be done to me? What is my responsibility to my family and friends? And also what is my responsibility to others, perhaps to people I don't even know?

The same questions apply to the widespread use of other **harmful drugs.** There are many ways to damage our bodies and diminish what life can hold.

Responsibility Toward Others

In the Apostle Paul's day the issue was meat that had been offered to idols (1 Cor. 8).

Mature Christians knew that idols did not have any real power. But weaker Christians weren't so certain.

If you **knew** an idol was only an object of stone or metal, if you were absolutely certain it had no meaning, what difference did it make if you ate such meat?

But Paul asks, what about the weaker brother or sister who sees you eating and because of your example is led back into idol worship?

The Brethren are not legalistic. There is no stern ironclad set of rules to force behavior.

We live in societies with many pressures to be less than God wants. Each of us, with "fear and trembling" (Phil. 2:13), needs to be aware of the awful choices before us. And each of us in love and confidence needs to find a way that for us seems to fulfill the high calling which Christ has placed before us.

To do: Give up one bad habit—smoking or drinking or overeating or staying up too late.

Some scriptures . . .

Life is more than material goods—Matthew 6:25–33
The foolishness of selfish seeking—Luke 12:16–21
When riches become too important—Matthew 19:16–23
The need to share—Luke 16:19–31
Seeing God among the poor—Matthew 25:31–46
Your body is a temple—1 Corinthians 6:19–20
The way to life is narrow—Matthew 7:13–14
The Christian is not given to excess—Galatians 5:19–25
We have responsibility to others—1 Corinthians 8:1–13
In baptism we have crucified lusts and desires—Romans 6:1–4
Christians use good language—Ephesians 5:4

12

"For We Are Saved by Grace Through Faith"

The challenge of Christ to his disciples was, "Be thou perfect" (Matthew 5:48). They were to "reach for the stars." To live God's life in a dirty world.

Yet we are imperfect. The Scriptures tell us that all have sinned and fallen short of the glory of God (Rom. 3:23; 5:12). Isaiah tells us that before God, even our righteousness is as "filthy rags" (Isa. 64:6).

We fail. Even the best of us fail. And the person who feels otherwise is perhaps the most guilty of all. More than obvious sins, Jesus condemned the sins of the heart. He was most critical of those who held heads aloof and thanked God that they were not like others (Luke 18:11).

The Church of the Brethren believes that all war is sin. Yet the church loves and supports all members and upholds for each the right of conscience. After any war, it attempts to welcome home those who have opposed the war and those who have fought in it. It seeks to draw them in with the same love and concern.

The church believes that divorce is wrong. One man, one woman in marriage for life. But the reality of our world is that there is divorce. And so the Church of the Brethren reaches out with amazing acceptance and compassion to those whose lives have been torn apart by divorce. It draws the hurting ones to itself to help them find healing and wholeness once again.

The Church of the Brethren believes that abortion is wrong. But the Brethren have refused to condemn or expel struggling human beings in an imperfect and immoral world who turn to abortion.

One of the distinguishing things about the Brethren is that they take Jesus very seriously. And one of the things this has meant for them is that they learn from Jesus a love which reaches out to accept and love others with whom they may disagree, to accept and love people who may have failed, to accept and love even people who have made mistakes and have done wrong.

Love Toward a Hated Killer

In the 1920s, the newspapers were filled with the story of the thrill killing of little Bobby Franks. Two bright, rich, young Jewish youth, Richard Loeb and **Nathan Leopold**, living in Chicago, set out to commit the perfect crime. They chose a boy they did not know, Bobby Franks. They killed him and expected to so cover what they had done that they would never be discovered.

But they were discovered and were brought to trial. The newspapers of the day carried headlines screaming for their deaths in payment. The entire nation seemed aroused.

The famous criminal lawyer, Clarence Darrow, took their case. He secured the verdict of "life plus 99 years."

Richard Loeb never changed. He was killed in a knife fight on the prison yard.

But Nathan Leopold was truly sorry. He asked forgiveness for his crime. He used his time in prison to study. He especially read everything he could in the field of medicine.

Years later officials announced that he was rehabilitated and asked for his parole. Leopold was asked to submit a list of places where he would want to serve. At the top of his list was the hospital of the Church of the Brethren in Castañer, Puerto Rico.

His request was granted.

My sister and her husband, a medical doctor, were on the staff of that hospital at Castañer at the time. They came to be close friends with Nathan Leopold.

In Puerto Rico at Christmas time, "Santa" did not bring the presents. A Wise Man, after the biblical story, brought the toys. Nathan Leopold became the Wise Man to bring the Christmas presents to the home of their little family.

A Love We Never Earn

At the heart of the Christian gospel is the good news that God loves us no matter what. No matter how bad we are, no matter how far we sink below what we ought to be. God loves us.

And at the heart of the gospel is the message that God can forgive us and make us new. We can be washed, forgiven, restored, and made into new creatures.

We do not earn salvation. God makes many demands. Salvation is not cheap. But we cannot buy it. It is a free gift from God. None of us deserves it. Salvation is God's gift given to us as we are ready to accept it. (Romans 5:15)

Perhaps as important as anything the Brethren have to offer is a warm, loving, caring fellowship of people who try to reflect that free gift of God.

For many, more than anything else, it is that warmth and acceptance, that taste of the kind of relationship which God wills for all people everywhere, that draws them into it. Not because of who we are, but in spite of who we are, God's love reaches out to us. And we, in turn, seek to open our lives to share that warmth and that love with others.

In God's eyes, that is surely more important than any theological system or doctrine or ideals to which we may cling.

To do: Show love to someone who seems unloved. Befriend one friendless person.

Some scriptures . . .

Though your sins are as scarlet—Isaiah 1:18
While we were yet sinners—Romans 5:6–21
The forgiveness of Jesus—John 8:2–11
The struggle to love and accept Saul—Acts 9:1–22
God's love for the lost—Luke 15
We are saved by grace through faith—Ephesians 2:8

13

Cathedrals of Love

Some churches, when construction is finished, are complete. Finished. The lines are such that many churches are all tied neatly together, perfect in every detail, nothing more could be done.

But gothic cathedrals were never finished. The lines soared toward something never ever completed.

Gothic cathedrals were built with limited funds. It was assumed that they would require generations of work. Gothic cathedrals depended on those who came after them to continue working on the dream, extending their work.

God calls us to be building cathedrals in the gothic style, not with short-term goals easily accomplished.

God calls us to long-term goals which are never fully accomplished.

God does not call us to be gothic cathedrals of stone and mortar, stained glass windows and massive pipe organs.

God calls us to build cathedrals of love, unfinished churches in our communities which are always reaching out, which are always incorporating new lives, which are full of people whose journey is never complete.

Long ago, Augustine said we are to be "perfect pilgrims. Not yet perfect possessors."

Sense of Community

The New Testament church was a close-knit family of believers. The early Christians ate, sang, talked, worshipped, and prayed together. They witnessed even to death together.

The early Brethren grew out of a strong sense of community.

From the outset, the Biblical faith was a faith of covenants. Abraham entered into a covenant with God and left his home, his family, his land, and headed out for a strange, unfamiliar, new land which God would give him (Gen. 12:1–9; Heb. 11:8–10).

The Hebrew people entered into a covenant with God. The theme of "covenant" is throughout the Old Testament. And the New Testament represents a new covenant between God and a much expanded faith family.

The New Testament people of faith were not in and out of that relationship. They did not live independent from each other. They belonged to each other and found meaning in their life together.

For Brethren, a strong sense of a covenantal community is important. Those new to the Brethren notice that it is like joining a new family. There are expectations. There is also much love and help.

Food and Song

From colonial times in America, the early Brethren were in the printing business. It is no accident that two of the all-time best selling books printed across the years were hymnals and the *Inglenook* cookbooks.

European research reveals that the first Brethren hymnal was printed in 1720, just twelve years after the church was begun.

Some of the hymns were written by people imprisoned for their faith. The music is of the finest quality of its time.

Across the years, Brethren have produced a number of poets and hymn writers. Singing has been an important part of their faith. In this they are like the early Christian church for which singing was a central part of their worship (Acts 16:25; Eph. 5:19; Col. 3:16).

Eating together has been another distinguishing mark of the Brethren. Like the early Christian church which ate together virtually every time they came together, meals have played a strong role in binding the church together (Acts 2:46; 1 Cor.

11:20). Taking time to sit and eat and have fellowship has deepened the bonds the Brethren have felt toward each other.

Aspects of Worship

There are some informal aspects of worship that are a part of the Sunday morning service for many Brethren. Many congregations have come to have a weekly segment called "The sharing of Joys and Concerns." Often the pastor will come down to the people and invite the congregation to share in prayer concerns and discoveries. It is a time for the gathered community to share their joys and sorrows.

People new to the church comment on the inclusion of children in many worship services. A children's story is not required but often is included in the order of worship in many Churches of the Brethren.

Frequently, the pastor will participate informally in aspects of the worship in a way that may not happen in other churches, like singing with the choir for their anthem.

A Practical, Downhome Faith

D. W. Kurtz, brilliant former president of Bethany Seminary, in 1933, wrote an article for the *Gospel Messenger* entitled "Ideals of the Church of the Brethren." He mentioned the usual things: peace, simple living, a rejection of things that are harmful to our bodies, reaching out to all races. He also mentioned "the good life," a belief that religion which issues from Jesus will be concerned about simple things like how we live the rest of the week.

In Quarryville, Pennsylvania, in the mid-1900s, an unpaid and very popular Brethren minister, **Rufus Bucher**, stated the Brethren understandings in plain and simple language. A stranger asked him if he were saved. His response was: "Ask my wife, my children, my neighbors." When evangelistic groups with animated singing and wild and loud worship began to spread in those parts, Bucher's response was, "I don't care how high they jump as long as they walk straight once they come down to earth."

Ronald C. Arnett, as academic dean at Manchester College, spoke to a group of students at Bethany Theological Seminary. He summarized the Brethren understanding very simply. He said: "We have a Church with a practical theology. As (the New Testament book of) James suggests, work hard, hold your tongue, take care of those less fortunate, and do not doubt the power of God. Our practical theology came from rural and blue collar roots. We are concerned about doing something, being practical with a faith. Our rural and blue collar ties call us to question a faith without action. Our spirituality is at its best not in the solitude of a closed room but in the heartbeat of the marketplace—living what we believe."

Ronald Arnett says that such an approach to religion has great appeal in Europe. There would be wide acceptance of our faith if we were willing to begin to share it. Interest in the Brethren understanding of the gospels comes from other parts of the globe as well.

Persons from Latin America, Indonesia, the Philippines, Japan, Korea, and elsewhere have been drawn to a church which seeks to have a strong evangelical faith combined with a strong concern about justice and peace.

One Third World person said, "The Church of the Brethren is uniquely a Third World Church." Among the elements some have seen are a clear sense of family and fellowship as well as a strong Biblical faith with definite social concern.

Wherever the Brethren have gone overseas, lives have been changed in significant ways.

In Ecuador

Raul Tasiguano was the youngest son of the first family baptized by Brethren missionaries in Ecuador. Raul attended the Brethren mission school and an agricultural college and returned to serve his home community. Back home, he became the inspired co-leader of a nonviolent protest of Quechua Indians in the rural Llano Grande community of Ecuador in 1970. A competitive (white) bus cooperative attempted to dominate the only transportation service to Quito where many of the Quechua Indians worked. The Indians were the object of segregation and abuse. The teaching of the Brethren led the Indians to insist on being treated fairly. In the end justice was gained for the Indians and the monopoly of the bus service was broken. Raul's efforts eventually caught the attention of even the president of Ecuador. The effort was successful, but on March 18, 1971, Raul was deliberately pursued, beaten, and run over twice by a bus on his way home from a community meeting. Raul was twenty-four when he died from his injuries.

In China

In 1908, our church began sending missionaries to China. More than 100 missionaries served, not only in evangelistic work but in medical work, education, agricultural extension, and industrial cooperatives. They did rural service and relief work in war torn areas after the Japanese invasion: soup kitchens, orphanages, nurseries, and medical units. Brethren Service sent tractor units in order to teach the Chinese to farm large areas of land.

With the takeover of the Communists, the curtain closed around China. For years, Brethren felt the effort in China had been without results. But with the US's recognition of Mainland China, the curtain began opening again. To our surprise, the church was still alive in China. **Yin Ji Zeng** was the son of the first Chinese minister ordained by the Church of the Brethren. He became one of the leaders in the Chinese protestant church. He served as pastor of the Rice Market Street Church in Beijing which the George Bush family attended when Mr. Bush was the US's chief liaison officer to China. Pastor Yin baptized the Bush's youngest daughter, Dorothy. China was a failed effort, years of sacrifice and service for nothing . . . we thought. Who would have guessed that a product of that mission would be the one to baptize the daughter of a future president of the United States!

Choices Before Us

In the past, the Church of the Brethren has grown strong as it has focused on great challenges. During the 1900s, the church developed a series of thirty-three camps and retreat centers across the United States. Later, in the early 1950s, it began to develop some twenty-two retirement centers and hospitals for its older members, offering a range of services from independent living to skilled nursing care, across the United States. Some are among the finest in the United States.

But other kinds of challenges were also taking place, world challenges. There were, first, overseas missions. Later, during and following World War II, there emerged Brethren Service and a worldwide program of relief and rehabilitation.

Today God may be calling the Church of the Brethren to leap beyond its national barriers.

Before his church became Brethren, **Abe Park,** a Korean Church of the Brethren pastor in Laguna Hills, California, was anxious as to how his people would receive the love feast. It seemed so much against the mood of his own native land.

But once his people experienced the love feast for the first time, he virtually exploded with enthusiasm. He said of that experience: "It is a spark to start a wildfire across Korea!" He felt the values Christ taught in that experience are the values most needed in his land today.

A student from Indonesia who was attending Bethany Theological Seminary was worried about being allowed to survive with Brethren values in his country. To talk of peace is to be viewed as a Communist, he said. But he, too, was convinced that the message is needed.

In 1980, **Jorge Toledo,** of the Vega Baja Church in Puerto Rico, responded to the devastation of Hurricane David in the Dominican Republic. He worked in the daytime rebuilding homes. At night he answered questions as to why he had come. He began baptizing and some communities of Christians were brought together, some in isolated villages that had no Christian presence before. Ten years later there were nine fellowships, three of them organized churches. Jorge says this is only a beginning and will spread to other places in the Caribbean Rim and on to Latin America.

Our theme in this chapter applies not only to congregations. The Church of the Brethren is also like a gothic cathedral, never completed, always changing, always growing as it seeks to do the will of God and to follow in Jesus' steps.

Tomorrow Is Already Here

Many are convinced that the best years for the Church of the Brethren lie ahead, not behind. God is calling us to rediscover and reaffirm what has been the cluster of convictions of our past.

From many lands people are saying, "Come over to Macedonia and help us" (Acts 16:9). Voices from other countries, who perceive our understanding of Christianity to be so much more than they find in its present forms in their lands, want us to join hands with them as equals. "As strangers no more but members of one family," they want us to work with them in helping the Church of the Brethren emerge in their own countries. They look toward a day when there will be world conferences of various Church of the Brethren national bodies.

You and I will play an important part in determining whether that happens.

The Imperative to Share

Romans 10:10 makes it clear that salvation is not complete until it is shared. "For it is by our faith that we are put right with God. It is by our confession that we are saved." Romans 10:9 says, "If you confess that Jesus is Lord and believe that God raised him from death, you will be saved." The Christ we will not share we cannot keep. The faith we would hoard, we lose. To witness to our faith is a vital part of what it means to be a Christian.

New Symbol for the Brethren

Earlier we mentioned the seal attributed to Alexander Mack, Jr. In 1987, a new logo was developed for the Brethren. It is very much like the Mack symbol. The cross at the heart of our faith recalls our baptism into Christ's death and resurrection (Rom. 6:4). The circle, partially shown, represents the world into which we are sent by Christ (Matt. 28:19). The wave reminds us of the waters of justice (Amos 5:24), the cup of water offered in Christ's name (Mark 9:41), and the basin and towel (John 13:5).

Perhaps someday around the world this new, simple symbol of the cross, the world, and the waters of righteousness and justice will begin to appear, bearing witness to indigenous Churches of the Brethren which have taken their clue from Jesus and are again bringing together the full gospel—the personal salvation we find in Jesus Christ and the call to be in the world, healing and teaching and bringing peace and justice and new life in his name.

To do: Could your congregation host an ethnic group which might be led into the Church of the Brethren? Explore the possibilities.

Some scriptures . . .

The gift is life—John 10:10

As the Father sent me . . .—John 20:19–21
For such a time as this—Esther 4:12–15
Salvation is only complete—Romans 10:8–10
To all peoples—Matthew 28:16–20.

Some Facts About the Church of the Brethren

Headquarters: Church of the Brethren General Offices
1451 Dundee Avenue
Elgin, Illinois 60120
Telephone: 800-323-8039

Seminary: Bethany Theological Seminary
Butterfield and Meyers Road,
Oak Brook, Illinois 60521
Telephone: 708-620-2200

Colleges: Bridgewater College
Bridgewater, Virginia 22812 .
703-828-2501

Elizabethtown College
Elizabethtown, Pennsylvania 17022
717-367-1151

Juniata College
Huntingdon, Pennsylvania 16652
814-643-4310

Manchester College
North Manchester, Indiana 46962
219-982-5000

McPherson College
McPherson, Kansas 67460
316-241-0731

University of LaVerne
LaVerne, California 91750
714-593-3511

The Brethren colleges offer a program entitled Brethren Colleges Abroad, the opportunity for study for a year or for a semester at:

The University of Barcelona, Spain;

The College of St. Paul and St. Mary in Cheltenham, England;

Dalian Foreign Language Institute in Dalian, China;

Hokusei University in Sapporo, Japan;

The University of Marburg, Germany; and

The University of Strasbourg, France.

For information contact:

Brethren Colleges Abroad, Manchester College, North Manchester, Indiana 46962, (219) 982-5000

The Church of the Brethren operates 25 hospitals and retirement homes in the United States.

The Church of the Brethren owns and operates 36 camps in the United States.

Brethren Service Center

Brethren World Peace Academy

Brethren World Peace Book Store

SERRV Headquarters
Box 188, New Windsor, Maryland 21776
Telephone: 301-635-6464

Brethren Service European Office
150 Route de Ferney
1211 Geneva 2
Switzerland

Church of the Brethren Washington Office
110 Maryland Avenue NE, Box 50
Washington, D. C. 20002
Telephone: 202-546-3202

Publications: *Messenger* (official monthly publication)
1451 Dundee Avenue
Elgin, Illinois 60120

Brethren Life and Thought (a quarterly, scholarly journal)
c/o Bethany Theological Seminary
Myers and Butterfield Roads
Oak Brook, Illinois 60521

Index

A

Abortion, 76
Abraham, 70, 80
Abstinence, 72
Alcohol, 73
Alcoholic, 30
Alternative Service, 52
Anabaptists, 15
Annual Conference, 12, 35 - 37,
        59, 64
Anointing, 27 - 31
Arab, 53
Armenians, 55
Arnett, Ronald C., 81
Arnold, Gottfried, 5
Association of Brethren
        Caregivers, 58
Augustine, 79

B

Baptism, 15 - 20, 30, 34, 74, 85
Barwick, John, 53
Beijing, 83
Bernard of Clairvaux, 11
Bethany Theological Seminary,
        81, 84, 87, 89
Biafrans, 52
Blacks, 59, 64 - 66
Blood, 10, 23, 25, 47 - 48, 61,
        63 - 64, 67
Bosler, Bill, 58 - 59
Bosler, SueZann, 59
Bread and Cup, 24 - 25
Brethren Service, 55 - 58, 62, 83,
        88
Brethren Volunteer Service, 56
Bucher, Rufus, 81
Buddhist, 61
Bura, 66
Bush, Dorothy, 83
Bush, George, 83

C

Callahan, Wanda, 60
Camps, 51, 53, 83, 88
Castañer, 76
Chesterton, G.K., 53
Child Dedication, 19
China, 66, 83, 88
Church of the Brethren, 1, 3,
        5 - 6, 14, 24, 35, 38 - 39,
        47, 54, 58 - 62, 64, 66,
        75 - 76, 81 - 85, 87 - 88
Church World Service, 56 - 57
Civil Rights, 64-66
Civil War, 64
Civilian Public Service, 51
Commissions, 37
Congregational Business
        Meeting, 37
Constantine, 47 - 48
Cornelius, 63
Councils of Churches, 56
Covenant, 11 - 12, 80
CROP, 57
Cuba, 56
Cyprus, 56

D

Darrow, Clarence, 76
David, King, 48
Denmark, 66
Dilling, Yvonne, 56
District Board, 37
District Conference, 37
Divorce, 75 - 76

E

Ecuador, 66, 82
Eder River, 3
El Salvador, 56
Europe, 82

Index of
Scripture References

Some Questions for Discussion

The most important questions are those which grow out of the reading. For the discussion of each chapter, begin by looking at three questions brought by each member of your discussion group.

In addition, you may want to consider such questions as these.

Chapter 1—Counting the Cost

1. Contrast a faith which begins with "an exclusive attachment to Jesus with a faith tested by the words of a creed.

2. Are there things in our day where following Christ will involve cost for us? List some. Discuss.

3. In your own Christian life, can you list new areas of belief or practice which have developed as you tried to follow Christ?

4. Why is belonging to a Christian group important?

5. Discuss the implications of the statements "the entire world belongs to God" and "as followers of Jesus we must seek God's will for every area of life." Can you think of any area of life where God is not concerned?

Chapter 2—Gathered Around the Word

1. Borrow Bibles from two people who underline as they read. You might ask your pastor to obtain Bibles from two people who are very different in their outlook, although both are dedicated Christians. Compare the parts that each has underlined. In some cases does the underlining of one stop where the other begins? What does this say about our willingness to receive all that God wants to say to us?

2. Ask three individuals to each read about one of the following: Bernard or Francis or Peter Waldo. Have each present some stories or information which tell us how their lives represented values important to the Brethren.

3. Some groups argue over whether we go to heaven when we die or later, at the end of time. They argue over whether Jesus said: "I say to you, this day you will be with me in Paradise." Or was it, "I say to you this day, you shall be with me in Paradise" (Luke 23:43). Jesus himself avoided such discussions (See Mat. 22:23–33; Mark 12:18–27; Luke 20:27–38). Jesus said in effect that God is faithful. God is Lord of life and death. Life after death will be good because, here or there, we are in the hands of a loving Creator. Can we be satisfied with Jesus? Or must we know more than Jesus felt we were ready or able to handle? (Read and discuss what Jesus meant in Matthew 22:23–25.)

4. Some years back when the Revised Standard Version of the Bible first appeared, in some areas of the United States copies were gathered up and burned because it translated Isaiah 7:14 as "young woman" rather than "virgin." Brethren looked at their German Bibles, saw that they gave the German word for "maiden," and refused to take part in the angry arguments. The Greek translation in the New Testament in RSV and in German read "virgin" (Matthew 1:23). Brethren, even in the most conservative churches, sensed that the issue was not one of the uniqueness of Jesus but of being faithful scholars. Discuss the difference between those who argue over fine details and those who seek the larger message God has for us.

5. Is there acceptance in your group for those of differing views? Is there freedom for people to find their way?

Chapter 3—Believers' Baptism

1. Does the issue of baptizing believers versus baptizing infants matter today? Why or why not?

2. Are unbaptized babies lost?

3. What is the difference between a sacrament and an ordinance?

4. What difference does being baptized make?

Chapter 4—The Love Feast

1. How do you feel about participating in footwashing?

2. Do you feel the idea of humble service is basic to being a Christian?

3. Does your culture honor servants?

4. Today do we feel the greatest are the servants of all?

5. Do we feel a strong sense that we belong to each other as Christians?

6. Contrast the bread and the cup as a sacrament with the idea that they symbolize letting Christ's life find expression in us.

Chapter 5—Anointing for Healing

1. Contrast popular "faith healing" with the anointing service. What are the differences?

2. In your experience can you share instances where "garbage" in a life prevented healing?

3. If "salvation" means wholeness, what kind of healing does God desire?

4. Does wholeness always mean physical health?

Chapter 6—The Priesthood of All Believers

1. Define "priests" in the phrase "we are to be priests to one another." What does this mean?

2. If "every member is a minister," how would our church life change?

3. Discuss your feelings about the leadership role of women in the church.

4. Contrast the organization of the Brethren where people share in decision-making with churches where one or a few people make the decisions.

Chapter 7—To Let Him Live in Us

1. What does the phrase "no creed but Christ" mean?

2. Has your faith grown or changed in the last year? If so, how?

3. Which is more important to you, the personal or the social aspect of the gospel?

4. In which area is your congregation stronger?

5. In which area does it need strengthening?

6. Consider these terms:

Some Churches	Some Other Churches
justice	judgment
social	personal
ecumenical	evangelical
relevant	biblical
social structures	sin
consultation	conversion
deprived	depraved
dialogue	decision
Christian faith	Jesus Christ
power	piety

Which is right? Or do both columns have elements which are essential? For Brethren, both columns are important. Underline the ones which need more attention from you if the whole gospel is to direct your life.

Chapter 8—All War Is Sin

1. We have no evidence that any Christian went to war for the first 300 years. List the teachings in the Gospel that might have led early Christians to this position.

2. Silently read Matthew 5:38–48. Discuss what this passage meant to people in Jesus' day. What does it mean to us if we take Jesus seriously?

3. Discuss alternative service and ways in which your church could help your youth know about alternatives to war and about Brethren Volunteer Service.

4. Brethren have been active in Councils of Churches both to share their faith and to receive insights from other Christians. Discuss your fears, convictions, and reactions to sharing in Councils of Churches.

Chapter 9—The Cup of Cold Water

1. Discuss: You can give and not love, but you cannot love and not give.

2. Brethren have been active in Councils of Churches both to share our faith and to receive insights from other Christians. Discuss your fears, convictions, and reactions to sharing in Councils of Churches.

3. Share stories you know of Christians who have served in significant ways.

4. What are the opportunities for service in your own community? Are there areas where you and your church should be involved?

Chapter 10—Of One Blood

1. Do you have prejudice?

2. Who are the most unaccepted people in your community? What is the responsibility of Christians?

3. How do you deal with prejudice in your own heart?

4. What are the areas where a "John Kline" is needed today.

Chapter 11—Stewards of God's Good Gifts

1. What would it mean to live the "simple life" today? List some changes you might make in your own life.

2. How do you feel about giving a tithe to Christ through your congregation?

3. If we really believed that the entire earth belongs to God, would we be better "stewards" of it? Name some specific areas needing attention.

4. Talk about what changes for "moderation in things good; abstinence from things harmful" might mean in your life.

Chapter 12—"For We Are Saved by Grace Through Faith"

1. Is it possible to hold strong convictions but still love and accept those who fail?

2. Talk about your feelings of acceptance and concern about:

homosexuals

those who have had an abortion

someone who has committed murder

a thief

a divorcee

3. Can you really believe that you, too, fail and are in need of God's love?

4. Is it easier for those who fail dramatically to believe in the need for humility and God's forgiveness? Read Luke 7:36–47. Discuss verse 47. What does this mean for those who feel they have been good people all their lives?

Chapter 13—Cathedrals of Love

1. Suggest some changes that might need to happen in your congregation if you were to become a "Cathedral of Love." Suggest some changes that might need to happen in yourself.

2. Is there a strong sense of commitment in your church? Are people "in and out" or are they constant in their love and devotion? How could a sense of community and commitment to each other and to Christ be deepened?

3. Discuss the idea of reaching out to other cultures and other nations. As more people come, the nature of the church will change. As mentioned, as the Apostle Paul headed out to preach to non-Jews, the church at Jerusalem worried that one day there would be "more of them than there are of us," and the church would change. There did, and the church did. Should that worry us? If so, why? Are there answers to our fears?

4. What is your vision for the next twenty-five years for our denomination? What should our church become?